MW00579539

JESUS *on the* JOB

Sharing your faith in the workplace

by Randall Farrell

Jesus on the Job: Sharing Your Faith in the Workplace
Copyright © 2021 by Randall Farrell

Randall welcomes comments, feedback, and queries (including questions about permissions to use quotes from this book) at the following email address: **randofarrell@gmail.com.**

All rights reserved. Except for brief quotations in printed reviews, no part of this publication may be reproduced, stored in a retrieval system, or transmitted in any form or by any means (printed, written, photocopied, visual electronic, audio, or otherwise) without the prior permission of the publisher.

Scripture taken from the New King James Version®. Copyright © 1982 by Thomas Nelson. Used by permission. All rights reserved.

Print Edition ISBN 13: 978-1-7332344-9-8
Kindle and ePub Editions ISBN: 978-0-57892-818-0

Cover designed by Noah Craig
Editing and interior design by Rick Steele Editorial Services
    (https://steeleeditorialservices.myportfolio.com)

Printed in the United States of America

Contents

There are very few books on the market that discuss the topic of sharing your faith in the workplace, and a practical "how to" resource is needed. Today's world is becoming more and more secular, and our laws are moving more toward prohibition of any expression of one's belief, faith, or worship. Actually, on second thought, here in the USA, it seems federally permissive to express one's belief and theory if you are speaking of any system other than Christianity. If you verbally disagree with Judaism, you are labeled antisemitic. If you speak against Islam, you must be Islamophobic. If you disagree with Eastern religions, you are xenophobic. My own opinion is that this trend is due to a supernatural influence from Satan that promotes the preaching of these non-Christian religions because there is no power in the names of these other deities and beliefs. But there is power in the name of Jesus. Power to heal, to change lives, and most importantly—to save souls! There is no need for Satan to attack other belief systems, because they do not lead to salvation. Yes, laws have been written to protect people from being harassed in the workplace by someone preaching and proselytizing regardless of that person's spiritual reference, and company policies generally do the same, but you seldom see people

1

being disciplined or steps being taken to prevent the spreading of spiritual teaching—only when someone is preaching the gospel of Jesus Christ.

It is important to note that I believe it to be proper Christian conduct to obey the rules and laws of the government and your employer. Hebrews 13:17 says: *"Obey those who rule over you and be submissive."*

I know, this verse refers to spiritual leadership, but it applies to secular leaders as well, because God puts all authority in place for His purpose. We should not do things against the law or policies of our employer. So how do we do that and still be bold for the gospel? That is what this book is about.

What are my credentials for writing such a book? At the time of this writing, I am in my 39th year with a Fortune 50 company. The name of the company is not important for reasons I will explain in a later chapter. For most of my career, I have been in a middle-manager position. I have led departments that range from eleven employees to eleven hundred. Most of my experience has been in manufacturing factories, but I did manage a field service organization for five years.

Spiritually, I was raised in a very religious home. We attended church each Sunday with few exceptions. I recall once when my dad was moving to a different job in a different city, he was speaking at his going-away party. He said the thing he was most proud of was the fact that he had raised five successful, God-fearing children. Our home was full of religious articles, and I was raised with the common clichés such as "thank the Good Lord above." While in high school, my parents seemed permissive in allowing me to miss church. Around that time, my family made what would be the last move we would make together. After this move, we just didn't seem to connect with a local church, and there was only one church in our denomination in that town. While in college, I began to grow skeptical of the doctrines of the denomination in which I was raised. As a biology major, I even doubted the existence of God. You see, I used to be an intellectual and was just too smart to believe the whole supernatural agenda of a supreme being that spoke earth and life into existence. Besides, I was learning an alternative to the creation theory. It was in my sophomore year that I stopped going to church, but I recall being afraid to actually say the words "there is no God." I know now that it was the Holy Spirit sealing me, protecting me, and preserving me for God's plan and purpose for my life. I am beginning to develop a weird theory that there is no such thing as atheists, only those who refuse to acknowledge what has been divinely revealed to them.

Romans 1:18–22 says:

"For the wrath of God is revealed from heaven against all ungodliness and unrighteousness of men, who suppress the truth in unrighteousness, because what may be known of God is manifest in them for God has shown it to them. For since the creation of the world His invisible attributes are clearly seen, being understood by the things that are made, even His eternal power and Godhead, so that they are without excuse, because, although they knew God, they did not glorify Him as God, nor were thankful, but became futile in their thoughts, and their foolish hearts were darkened. Professing to be wise, they became fools."

My girlfriend, now my wife of forty years, asked me to attend a non-denominational church that she had been attending. Out of my desire to please her, I attended. It was a transient church that did not even have membership. It was a place to come and worship and hear the Word preached without structure or denominational influence. Even though

I am very active in a denominational system now and support denominational structure as a way of organizing mission work and sound theology, this church was just the place I needed at the time to reacquaint myself with God. Susan and I were married in that church, and as I think back, the preaching was scripturally sound, but I don't think I really accepted the gospel message of salvation by grace through faith and not through my good works until we had moved away and joined a different church. I was saved and baptized at the age of 25 when I realized this was a free gift from God and all I had to do was accept it. My life verse became Ephesians 2:8–9: *"For by grace you have been saved, through faith, and not of yourselves: it is the gift of God, not of works, lest anyone should boast."*

Once the Holy Spirit revealed to me that I was still depending on being good to get me to heaven, these verses came alive. I don't recall but I probably smacked myself in the head and thought, *Oh, I get it now.* I still can't say that I had a momentary salvation experience like so many people have. With me it was more of a process. You can argue if that is possible if you like, but all I know is that I'm saved, and it doesn't matter if it happened over time or at 10:48 AM while sitting in Northside Christian Church in New Albany, Indiana, on July 16, 1983. The church is real; the time and date are made up, but you get the point.

I moved with my wife and daughter Samantha from New Albany to the New Orleans area in 1990. We attended a small independent Bible church in the town of Luling, Louisiana. We sat under a pastor that was a graduate of Dallas Theological Seminary. If you know about this renowned seminary, you know that their grads know the Bible and are generally great expository preachers. Roger Coulter was no exception.

He taught me so much about scripture and gave me conservative interpretation. I was discipled in that church and grew to the point that I was asked to be a deacon. I served in that role there and at two other churches in the North Georgia area. I have taught Sunday School for thirty-plus years as well. As mentioned before, I am in a denominational church now, which I am not ashamed of, but I hesitate mentioning it by name, because, as Christians, we are becoming fractured and divided by denominational differences and have resorted to putting labels on people.

Example: If I told the name of the denomination, you may immediately think, *Oh, he's one of those, and that means he believes this and that*, which may differ from your interpretation and make me and what I have to say in this book less than credible to you. All I know is that the church to which I belong, and the pastor, preach Christ crucified, and all else is somewhat peripheral. I stand by my convictions, which you would label conservative if you heard them, but this is not the topic of this book. You can use the examples I'm going to give no matter what your background or theological conviction, as long as it is Christian. More about that in the next chapter.

I thought it important to let the reader know my background and give a little of my testimony so that you will know who it is you are reading to be credible in your thoughts even if you disagree with something I write. Please note that my testimony is much longer than the synopsis of my professional career. That's on purpose, and it's important. This book is very much about treating the physical world as a manifestation of the spiritual realm. It is the spiritual, supernatural part of our lives that should influence the physical, not the other way around. I will refer back to my testimony in this writing because it is the experience that has brought me to this point in my life, considering myself successful with my testimony being the basis for my success.

This idea of the spiritual influencing the physical is in part the answer to the question, why this book? My observation is that so many Christians today are trying to wrap their spiritual walk around their jobs, families, hobbies, and trials of life, and it should be the other way around where the Word of God and our obedience to it is the core of our existence, and everything else should be wrapped around it—always returning to the core for explanation and guidance. You may be saying to yourself…

That sounds great Randall, but what in the world are you talking about?

We tend to evaluate our spiritual walk and then customize it to fit our physical lives. One example would be tithing or giving a tenth of our income to the church. We may say, "I would like to give, and I know it's important, but if I give a tenth, I will not have enough to live on."

I guess we don't believe Malachi 3:10: *"And try Me now in this, says the Lord of hosts, If I will not open for you the windows of heaven and pour out for you such blessing that there will not be room enough to receive it."*

We think that our physical needs are more important than our spiritual obedience to the Word. In the example of tithing, we need to give as the Lord commands and watch him take care of the physical.

You say, *But Randall, you don't understand…*

Sure, I do. Susan and I are tithers. We give a tenth of our gross income and then give to other causes on top of that.

Yeah, but on a manager's income, you can afford to do that.

Yes, we are blessed with a good income, but remember, a tithe is a percentage. If you only make a little, you only give a little. And I will also confess that we did not one day start giving a tenth. We prayed for the faith that is required to adjust our lifestyle to giving a tithe and built up to a place where we are giving a tenth of our gross. And as my 40-inch waist will testify, I've not missed too many meals by doing so. God has been faithful to provide.

But tithing is only one example of adjusting your life to what God commands. You may be thinking, *But I could get in trouble or even fired if I share the gospel at work.*

Yes, you could, but are you depending on the physical to take care of you or God?

"What then shall we say to these things? If God is for us, who can be against us?" (Romans 8:31)

I don't recall a time when I "got in trouble" for sharing my faith, but there were a few softball warnings thrown my way. I recall a few times when someone in leadership would make a point to mention our need to be inclusive of all people and their beliefs and that we should not have discussions or comments that may be offensive to anyone. I once told my manager, "One day, you will have to call me into your office and tell me I have to stop preaching." God blessed me with a manager that replied, "That will never happen." We did get a directive to not allow religious tracts to be distributed or made available in the facility because it may offend some people. This was very difficult for me, but I complied in order to submit to those in authority over me and because there are other ways to share the gospel. Some of the tracts that were being displayed did not contain solid theology, so I didn't mind confiscating them. This book is an attempt to show examples of how to share without getting in trouble, but even if we do, we must yield to a higher calling than our own self-preservation. Our spirit should convict and convince us that God will take care of us if we obey. I had a pastor once who gave me great advice when I asked him about submitting to our earthly masters when it conflicts with scriptural teaching. He told me that we should always follow scripture, but submission to our earthly masters (company, boss, government) may mean we have to experience the consequences for following God, such as fines, jail, or losing a job. Paul described how we should live in his second letter to the Corinthians…

"But in all things we commend ourselves as ministers of God: In needs, distresses, in stripes, in imprisonment, in tumults, in labors, in sleeplessness, in fasting, by purity, by knowledge, by longsuffering, by kindness, by the Holy Spirit, by sincere love, by the word of truth, by the power of God, by the armor of righteousness on the right hand and on the left, by honor and dishonor, by evil report and good report; as deceivers and yet true; as unknown and yet well known, as dying, and behold we live, as chastened and yet not killed, as sorrowful, yet always rejoicing, as poor yet making many rich, as having nothing and yet possessing all things." (2 Corinthians 6:4–10)

We should see ourselves in many parts of these passages. We will never be faced with the trials that beset Paul and the other apostles for the sake of Christ, but we also don't have the faith that Paul had to stand strong through these trials. Could it be that Paul actually saw Jesus and knew He was real and therefore had greater faith?

"Thomas, because you have seen me, you have believed. Blessed are those who have not seen yet they have believed." (John 20:29)

What does that say about our belief and faith? Our lack of faith is something that can be fixed but we have to make our spirit boss over our lives rather than our lives boss over our spirit.

So, I have taken you to two extremes, from the mild issue of tithing, which some consider to not be God's command at all but rather an Old Testament ritual meant only for the Jews, to the opposite extreme of losing your job and going to jail. I guess there is yet another level of extreme consequence, which is giving your life for the gospel of Christ as many of the early church did and as many are still doing today. So what are the things in the middle of these extremes that we may encounter every day? Things that require a decision...

Will I follow the Spirit and obey the Word of God or satisfy my flesh and do what will profit me in the physical realm?

The key is to ask "What would Jesus do?" Allow me to list some examples.

My coworker lost a parent this week, and I should probably go to him and encourage him, but he has not been very nice to me lately and I've heard he's been talking about me behind my back.

"See that no one renders evil for evil to anyone, but always pursue what is good both for yourselves and for all." (1 Thessalonians 5:15)

Many places in the Bible command us to be an encouragement to the brethren. What if the person is not a believer?

We'll cover that later. We should have a spirit of forgiveness and not be self-centered. We need to bring comfort where comfort is needed—no matter what our relationship is with the individual. This is what Jesus would do.

I'm tired of working my tail off for this company and not being appreciated, getting no recognition, and someone else getting praised for my work.

> *"...or whatever you do,*
> *do all to the glory of God."* (1 Corinthians 10:31)

We must remember, spiritually speaking, we are not working for our employers, we are working for God. God provided our jobs, and we are to glorify Him by the way we do it. We shouldn't complain that we are not recognized by our companies because we should be working to be recognized by God. If we are working for our self-promotion, we will fall to jealousy and bitterness. We must work hard to glorify God by our example regardless of our reward and recognition. Does God see the work you do? Yes! Does God appreciate the work you do? Yes, if you are doing your best and working hard to glorify Him. If you're not sure, maybe you should ask Him.

This is a dead-end job. I am capable of so much more, and I just can't get the break that will get me where I belong, a place to reach my potential.

> *"But as God has distributed to each one,*
> *as the Lord has called each one,*
> *so let him walk."* (1 Corinthians 7:17)

As much as you think you are driven by your own skill, ability, and ambition, you are not. You are called to be where you are in this season of your life, and you need to submit to God's plan for your life.

So, you say I should never go anywhere else or promote to a different job?

No, I'm not saying that. I'm saying that you need to ask God where He wants you to be.

If this company wants more out of me,
they can pay me more.

> *"And remain in the same house,*
> *eating and drinking such things as they give,*
> *for the laborer is worthy of his wages.*
> *Do not go from house to house."* (Luke 10:7)

The context of this passage is Jesus instructing the apostles as they go out to spread the gospel and do works in His name. Some may interpret this passage differently, but I see it as telling us to be satisfied with what God has provided for the work that He has called us to do. If He wants you to have more, He will bless you with a promotion and/or move your situation in some way that earns you more.

That other person makes more than me, and I do twice as much.

Do I really need to quote a scripture here about jealousy? Enough said!

I need to be all I can be and reach my potential.

Putting the spirit ahead of the physical means you need to be all God wants you to be while submitting to His will, which means you need to know what that is and be satisfied with His plan for your life. We need to buy in to the concept that His will for our life is much better than anything we can dream, fabricate or develop for ourselves.

I know God has put me here,
but I just can't do this anymore.

> "*I can do all things through Christ who strengthens me.*"
> (Philippians 4:13)

I was once at a point of burnout with work, family, and church service. On my prayer walk one morning, I was crying out to God to ease the pressure and stress. Instead of asking questions, I was making statements, telling Him I couldn't do this anymore, and since I couldn't give up my job or family, I would have to pull out of some of my church responsibilities. I returned home and declared I would just open the Bible randomly and read wherever it landed. I prayed that He would give me not guidance, but comfort in my situation. It happened to open to Job.

Wonderful! Job will understand what I am going through, I said to myself.

I randomly read from the top of the page, which was Job 40:7 in the NASB Bible: "*Now gird your loins like a man; I will question you and you will answer Me.*"

Not exactly what I wanted to hear, but it was what I needed. As I read on, I realized that God had given me great opportunity to make a great living, gave me a mission field at work, hold great responsibility, possess a huge toolbox of spiritual gifts to use for His kingdom, and most importantly, He had prepared and equipped me for the work. I just needed to be faithful and leave the results to Him. What a relief!

These are just examples of how we make the spiritual con-form to the physical when it should be the opposite. These examples reflect attitudes that I have heard in my career. I am ashamed to confess that some of these reflect attitudes I have exhibited in my career. I have a great testimony about submit-ting your career to the Lord that I will discuss in a later chap-ter. Because these attitudes exist even among Christians, we need a guide to help us reflect, bathe them with scripture and adjust our lives to fulfill what God desires for us. This book is an attempt to be that guide.

1

HOW?

Let's get started by making one thing very clear. The suggestions in this book are meant for those that are saved by the blood of Jesus. If you are not, you will not have the calling, the desire, nor the power of the Holy Spirit to share the gospel with others. Even if you claim to be Christian, you may not be. Christianity is not a label to be selected by individuals who want to identify with a church, denomination, or an ideology that does good things for people. Christian churches all over the world have people that have been attending for years but are not saved. I attended church for the first twenty-five years of my life and at times was very devout, but I was not saved.

So, what am I calling being "saved"? To be saved, you must confess to God that you are a sinner and that you cannot do anything to atone for your sins. You are in need of a Savior to atone for them. Jesus was and is that Savior, and His death on the cross is the atonement for all of our sins. You have to accept that sacrifice, His death on the cross, and resurrection, as the only way you can be forgiven of your sins and go to heaven. In giving your sins to Jesus and accepting His atonement, you are saved and have begun the process of making Him the Lord of your life.

So, how can I be so dogmatic about this?

You are a sinner and need a Savior. *"For all have sinned and fall short of the glory of God."* (Romans 3:23)

Jesus is your Savior. *"That if you confess with your mouth the Lord Jesus and believe in your heart that God has raised Him from the dead, you will be saved."* (Romans 10:9)

Jesus is the only way that you can be saved. *"Nor is there salvation in any other, for there is no other name under heaven given among men by which we must be saved."* (Acts 4:12)

"I am the way, the truth and the life. No one comes to the Father except through Me." (John 14:6)

You must accept salvation as a free gift of God, not something you have earned or achieved for yourself. *"For it is by grace you have been saved, through faith and that not of yourselves; it is the gift of God, and not of works lest anyone should boast."* (Ephesians 2:8–9)

You must accept this and only this for your salvation as a gift from God, that nothing else is needed. *"But as many as received Him, to them He gave the right to become children of God, to those who believe in His name: who were born, not of blood, nor of the will of the flesh, nor of the will of man, but of God."* (John 1:12–13)

The Basis for Belief

Maybe you don't believe the Bible is the Word of God without error. Some who call themselves Christians take the position that the Bible is good for general guidance but has contradictions and no longer fully applies to today's society or is allegorical in nature. If you have this opinion of the Bible you will struggle with what I have to say in this book, but I encourage you to read on.

Let's discuss the Bible for a moment, because it is the basis of all my arguments and this entire approach to sharing the gospel. If you don't believe the Bible, there is no gospel to share.

You may be thinking,

But Randall, I'm not saying I don't believe the Bible or the gospel of Christ, I'm saying I don't believe all of the Bible is literal, and it is certainly not contemporary.

> *"In the beginning was the Word,*
> *and the Word was with God and the Word was God.*
> *He was in the beginning with God."* (John 1:1–2)

You see, Jesus is the Word of God, so if you don't believe the Word, you don't believe Jesus.

Well, of course I believe Jesus.

Then you must believe the Word, the Bible. For if you don't believe all the Bible, you can't trust any part of it as truth, except for the parts with which you happen to agree. If you are picking and choosing what you believe, then your beliefs are not based on any standard. In short, you're just making it up.

We all strive to interpret scripture, thinking we have absolute truth and then later find reason to change our interpretation when we hear something different preached or the Holy Spirit reveals a different interpretation during our quiet time and/or Bible reading. This happens frequently, because God gives us all different amounts of faith depending on our desire to grow the faith that He has already given. We must exercise and grow our faith for the Holy Spirit to reveal truth to us.

"So then faith comes by hearing, and hearing by the Word of God." (Romans 10:17)

Not only do some self-claimed Christians not believe the Bible, but they do not necessarily believe Jesus was/is real. I was on a Facebook string of responses to a theological question once, and someone I didn't know gave the opinion, "Being Christian doesn't mean you are a follower of Jesus Christ. It is the way you live your life and help others."

Really?

The New Testament was originally written in Greek, and the Greek word for Christian is *Christianos*, which means "follower of the anointed." "The anointed" is Jesus. We must not allow society to redefine that which God has already defined in His Word.

As for the argument that the Bible no longer applies to modern-day society, I say...you're right, and that's the problem. The Bible should be applied to modern-day society, and we have numerous social issues because we don't apply biblical teaching. As for being called "old fashioned," I say "guilty as charged." The very newest of my ideas are two thousand years old, and they get older from there. My question is who had the authority to change or negate anything in the Word of God? The question is rhetorical, obviously, no one has that authority.

I feel it important to establish my reference for all that I'm writing. It's the Bible. Now we need to discuss the application of biblical principles to our lives, and specifically, sharing Jesus with others. If you are sharing the gospel, you will eventually need some familiarity with the scripture passages mentioned earlier. If you don't think these verses apply, I would encourage you to ask God to show you the truth about these passages and give you clear understanding of them and how they may be used to lead someone to Christ.

Uh oh! Time for semantics! Most Christian leaders use that term "lead someone to Christ." I understand what they mean, sharing with someone the gospel message and encouraging them to pray to receive Christ. Maybe even help them with the sinner's prayer. Technically speaking, I believe we cannot lead someone to Christ. It is Christ who draws us, calls us, and saves us.

"and no one can say Jesus is Lord except by the Holy Spirit." (1 Corinthians 12:3)

"(for the children not yet being born, nor having done any good or evil, that the purpose of God according to election might stand, not of works but of Him who calls)." (Romans 9:11)

"So then it is not of him who wills, nor of him who runs, but of God who shows mercy." (Romans 9:16)

You see, God seeks us and provides the very faith that brings us to Him for salvation. Don't get upset if you disagree; I only mention it because it will be important to remember as we discuss sharing your faith. Allow me to make peace by saying "saved is saved," and it makes little difference whether it was your choice or God's calling.

Lifestyle Evangelism

Since you are reading on, I am assuming you want to learn some different ways to share your faith in the workplace. Let's get started.

You need to examine your life to see if you reflect Christ in it. There is no need to be perfect; in fact, you will have more credibility with people if they see that you are normal, with flaws. It is hard to witness to someone who is turned off because your light shines too brightly. So, be real with people, and they will not as likely resent whatever holiness they see in you. It is important to know that there is a delicate balance between standing for holiness and presenting an offputting "holier than thou" attitude. Be aware, however, that if you are going to share your faith in public, especially in the workplace, you will need to be above reproach in all you do. Again, this does not mean perfection, but rather being above reproach. People will understand someone who is "good" in their eyes being human and having quirks, moments of failure, and lapses of judgment, but, if they appraise you as someone with character that is open, honest, and fair, they will respect you enough to overlook your infrequent shortcomings.

A key ingredient is having a genuine care for people. You've heard the saying "people don't care how much you know until they know how much you care." I have found this statement to ring true in my experience. There is no better way to show Christ in your life than to give care to someone without expectation of reciprocity. In a department of a thousand people, I know about five hundred by name and have a personal relationship with about one hundred. By personal relationship, I mean we talk frequently about things other than work, such as sports, family, our faith, and prayer needs.

We have a practice where I worked that when one of our employees has a death in the family, the department manager visits the employee at the funeral home. On average, I made one visit a week. I would go three or four weeks without a visit but sometimes have three or four in a week. I've even had three visits in a single night. It is out of these visits that many of these relationships are formed. People that I don't even know are blessed by the manager showing up. They are even more blessed when I share Christ with them. I usually ask if the loved one was saved. If they say yes, I can remind them of the comfort they can have knowing their loved one is with the Lord. If they say no, I tell them I am sorry, and I ask if they are saved. This can lead to a discussion about salvation. At a time of mourning, it needs to be short, but I introduce the idea to them and offer them the peace that surpasses all understanding and tell them that I will make myself available to them if they need to talk about it. This way, they are not offended, and the next step is theirs. If they seek me out for help, it is their choice, and I am not forcing anything on them. I've never had anyone complain that I preached at them during the visit, but I have had people tell me, "I saw what you were made of when you came to see me at the funeral home." I cannot count the number of people that, because of a visit, have stopped me in the factory and asked me to pray for a need that they have.

Showing Christ in your life by showing people you care about them is the best way to get them interested in why you care about someone you really don't even know. They may at a later time ask, "Why do you do that? Why are you like that?" This is precisely what you want, for someone to see a positive difference in you and ask you why. Once they ask, you can answer without fear of harassment charges because they asked, and you are just answering their question. The important thing to remember here is that you need to start at a high level and let them show an interest for more. I recall an employee once asked me just as a way of greeting,

"Randall, what do you know good?"

This is a common greeting in the South. The Holy Spirit was with me because I answered before I even thought of a response.

"I know I'm going to heaven when I die. That's good," I replied.

Some people come back with, "Amen, brother," when I give that response. This lady asked a deeper question.

"You mean you know that you are going to heaven?"

"Yes, I do," I said.

"How can you know?" she asked.

I shared Acts 16:31, *"Believe on the Lord Jesus Christ, and you will be saved."*

I also gave her some of the verses listed earlier. I told her I knew I was going to heaven when I died. Hey, she asked, so I get to answer. She told me she used to go to church but has not attended in many years. I told her where I attended and invited her to church and to my Sunday School class. She appreciated the invitation and said she may show up. She has yet to come but I frequently told her, "Hey, I'm still saving you a seat in class." She saw it as encouragement and not harassment. She now attends regularly at a different church of her choosing, which is fine, as long as she is attending.

God gives us the words when we are unable to come up with something profound at the needed moment. I call them "lightning strikes" because they happen without warning and without forethought. It's like the words come out of my mouth before I even think of them. That's how I know it was from God. I was in a meeting with about fifteen people once, and someone brought up the fact that our new vice president in our business group was only thirty-three years old and how amazing that was. Without thinking, I blurted out, "Well, Jesus was only thirty-three, and He saved the entire world."

I was greeted by silence and stares for a few moments, followed by general around-the-room agreements. This was a lightning strike, because at that point in my walk, I was not nearly that bold in sharing my faith.

Preparation

But Randall, this never happens to me, you may be thinking.

You may be right. It takes preparation. You must be someone that God chooses to work through by sending His words through your heart and mouth to someone He wants to reach at a particular moment. How can you be that someone? Have a relationship with Him so He can trust you to deliver the words and follow up. The lightning strike will be His words, but you need to be faithful to follow it up with your words, your experience, and your faith. I don't recall ever getting two lightning strikes immediately, back to back. This can be the scary part and why you need to be prepared, and the way you prepare is to be in fellowship with Him. This means a lifestyle of prayer and Bible reading and study. If you are going to share your faith, you need to know something about what you are sharing. This doesn't mean everyone must attend seminary and become a Ph.D in theology, but if you don't know that you are saved and why, and how, you are not ready to share. You get this information from listening to preaching, Sunday School discussions, group or independent Bible study, and through personal reading. When you get information from another person, remember that every person's words must be compared to scripture and that no person has all the answers. Interpretation of scripture is something we all need help with, and there are many people that are more qualified to interpret because of their formal education. It is great to have these people to interpret for us, but we should take the responsibility of learning as we grow so we can discern speakers and teachers that do not interpret scripture correctly.

"Be diligent to present yourself approved to God, a worker who does not need to be ashamed, rightly dividing the word of truth." (2 Timothy 2:15)

I actually heard a cleric say that she didn't believe that God condemns homosexuality in the Bible. She was not rightly dividing the word of truth even though she was a pastor prominent enough to be on a national TV show that had a panel of clerics from different faiths.

I will likely lose many readers at this point because you may think I am a "hater" and not rightly dividing the word of truth, myself. I will stop the homosexuality discussion here, because that is not what this book is about, but I will encourage you to prayerfully read your Bible.

My point here is that not everyone who is prominent and educated interprets the Bible accurately and properly. You have to discern truth. I really like reading and listening to John MacArthur. I think he is one of the best expositors of the Bible today, but I would not accept every word he preaches and teaches just because it is coming from John MacArthur. We need to prayerfully study the Word, so we know when we are being led astray.

The important thing to consider is whether you are ready to share your faith with others, especially the lost, until you know what your faith is. At times I am asked questions that have been the source of debate and arguments since Christ Himself walked the Earth. I don't pressure myself to be able to answer the mysteries of the faith, especially when I sense someone is just trying to pick a spiritual fight. Sometimes I have to just give the following answer:

"I don't know about that. All I know is that there was a man. His name was Jesus, He was God's Son, He came to

Earth in the flesh to fulfill God's plan of redemption for fallen man, and He died on the cross as a blood sacrifice to atone for my sin, and because I accept His death on the cross for the forgiveness of my sin, I am saved and will go to heaven when I die for all eternity."

"Yeah, but what about…?"

"I don't know about that. All I know is…"

It's not critical for you to be the world's greatest apologist (a defender of the faith); you just need to be able to present the gospel (see the "I don't know about that" quote above) and what it means in your life. If you have no witness, no message, no impact on your life that you recognize and can talk about, you have a faith issue and need to work on it.

I'm not trying to judge you or your faith; that's for you and God to do. I think it is important, however, to understand that you shouldn't be sharing a little bit of religious interest for reasons of being popular, show yourself as an insightful person, or to manipulate others by gaining their favor, pretending to have a common interest. I have heard many people after hearing me make some spiritual reference try to chime in with what they know of religion or the Bible. They sometimes butcher the scriptures or misapply them totally. I was speaking with a sales manager once on the topic of asking customers for a good rating on a survey. He was trying to get the group to ask for a good rating and he said, "Ask and you shall receive. Isn't that what the Bible says, Randall?"

I said, "Yes, but there's more to it than that."

He didn't take it any further, because he really didn't want to know. It was a rhetorical question. He was just trying to gain popularity by referring to a common biblical saying and make himself look like a moral person for doing so. How many times have you heard someone say, "The Lord helps those that help themselves"?

Actually, that's not in the Bible.

We need to strive for holiness. Yes, that means watching your language and the content of your discussions. Profane language and dirty jokes do not give you the credibility you need to share Christ with someone. I know people that are sincere Christians but have not learned to "tame the tongue." This doesn't mean they are not saved, but it does mean they are less effective in sharing their faith. I recall early in my career, before I was saved, I would speak frequently with someone and use profanity. He asked if I was a Christian, and I answered yes, not totally knowing what that meant. He said, "Well, I didn't know. I've heard you use some pretty rough language." He wasn't judging my salvation, he was inspecting my fruit. That made an impression on me and made me reflect on the image I was presenting. I wasn't sharing my faith in those days, but if I had, I wouldn't have had the credibility to do so.

"Let no corrupt word proceed out of your mouth, but what is good for necessary edification, that it may impart grace to the hearers." (Ephesians 4:29)

The Meaning of Life

We need to be sincere about the grace that saves us from eternal damnation to the point that we want to share it because of the good news we know it to be. That needs to be our motive along with the obedience we owe to God, for He has commanded us to share (see Matthew 28:19–20). Yes, we are commanded, but many of us try to give the excuse,

"My beliefs are private between me and God. I don't wear my spirituality on my sleeve for everyone to see."

Oh, beloved, you need to. You need to show you are different because you are a new creature in Christ. You serve a higher power than that which is on the Earth. You need to show you have died to self and no longer live, but Christ instead lives in you. You need to be a demonstration that Jesus can take an ordinary life guided by the love of the flesh and change it to one that seeks to glorify the Father. You may be the only Christ that some people ever see because there is no one else to exemplify Him. It is an awesome responsibility to carry but also an awesome privilege. God, the Creator of the universe, has chosen you to be the instrument by which someone will come to a saving knowledge of Jesus Christ and gain everlasting life. You can't top that with salary, benefits, acclaim, awards, or any kind of self-fulfillment; believe me, I've tried.

Wow, this is getting dangerously close to explaining the meaning of life!

It's not dangerously close, it's spot on. **This is the meaning and purpose of life, to accept Jesus and to glorify God by doing His will and telling people about Him.** Everything else we do is merely a way of fulfilling this purpose. I used to admire people that were on a mission to discover the meaning of life. How insightful, how intelligent, how inspiring I thought these people were! I now find it comical what some "enlightened" folks come up with for the meaning of life. They get so wrapped up in the *complexity* of the question, they refuse to acknowledge the *simplicity* of the answer. It's salvation, it's Jesus, it's glorifying God.

You may have heard a hypothesis such as,

The meaning of life is to channel your energy so that you create a positive karma that aligns with the energy of others to bring harmony to the world.

Or,

The meaning of life is to be all you can be, to reach your potential and contribute everything possible to society.

Sounds great, doesn't it? Unfortunately, it is as wrong as lips on a chicken.

Or how about,

The meaning of life is to help others and to feel good about yourself because you have done right.

Getting closer, but that is still about exalting ourselves rather than God. No, I'm going to stick with salvation, Jesus, and glorifying God. When Jesus' life was at an end, He prayed a summary of His mission and the meaning of His life.

"Father, the hour has come. Glorify Your Son, that Your Son may also glorify You." (John 17:1)

"I have glorified You on the Earth. I have finished the work which You have given Me to do." (John 17:4)

The take-away from this chapter should be:

Live your life as to glorify God so that people will want to know why you are different.

Prepare yourself so that you can be ready to tell others why you are different, because of Christ.

"But sanctify the Lord God in your hearts, and always be ready to give a defense to everyone who asks you a reason for the hope that is in you, with meekness and fear." (1 Peter 3:15)

CHAPTER

2

LET'S TALK ABOUT
THE JOB

So, we've talked about the way Christians should present themselves as those who show Christ in our lives and live our lives in a way that will make others admire us enough to ask why we are different. Some call this "Lifestyle Evangelism," which I think is a great term. Then you need to be ready to tell them why and defend the faith that you have and are demonstrating through the way you live your life and react to the issues of the world and your workplace.

Now let's talk about the job. Why are you in it? I will pause here and let you think about that for a few minutes.

Welcome back! If you made a list of reasons, lets discuss your list for a moment. Does your list look something like this?

- To provide for my family
- To reach my potential
- To utilize my education, skills and experience
- I enjoy this kind of work
- This job is very rewarding
- I deserve this job because of my hard work
- It pays well

- For the medical insurance and other benefits
- I'd be bored without a job
- It defines who I am
- I could not get a different one so I'm hanging on to this one
- I'm in too much debt to quit

These are common answers and certainly ones that I have used in the past. I can tell you that they are all wrong. If you are a Christian, you are in your job to be obedient to God's calling on your life and to glorify Him in the way you do it.

Wait a minute, I don't feel God calling me to be in this job.

Let's start there. God has a plan for your life. If your job is a major part of your life (and whose isn't?), then your job is probably part of that plan. You may not have asked God when you took your job but that doesn't mean He doesn't plan to use you in it for His purpose. Even if you didn't hear God's voice when you were deciding to take your job, He may have been calling you all the same. I'm quite sure I've missed God's calling more times than I've heard and obeyed it. I believe God sometimes calls you to a work, kingdom work, and lets you choose where to do that work.

Once in my career, I was prepared to leave secular work and go to work for a ministry. I thought that any ministry would want a manager that was trained by one of the world's greatest companies and was ready to go to work for a fraction of his current salary in order to serve God in his work. After sending out over one hundred résumés and not receiving so much as a note in return, I must tell you that I was quite dismayed.

"Father," I asked, "why won't You put me in a place where I can serve you more?"

After I prayed this for a few weeks I heard His answer.

"Randall, I have Christians in those ministries. I need a Christian in a secular job environment to minister there."

I realized then that working in a Christian organization was what *I wanted*. I was tired of swimming with the sharks. I wanted to work with people that had a Christian perspective. But I was focused on *my desires* and *my comfort* in *my work*. Once I submitted to God's will for my career, I was immediately presented with an opportunity that has brought me great rewards, financially as well as spiritually. I've been given several opportunities to witness and minister, and my boss was a true brother in Christ. We prayed together often, and he understood where I was coming from and allowed me to let Christ lead me in business decisions. I didn't know how God would be using me, but I trusted that He had a purpose for me being there and that I needed to obey that calling. I now see that I was there to encourage my boss to follow Christ in his job as well and apply biblical principles as he led the business. I also saw that I may be the only glimpse of Christ that some people see. I needed to show the joy of my salvation and give a reason for it. I also needed to be an encourager to those that were suffering with illness, family tragedy, addictions, or loss. I also needed to work very hard as if unto the Lord.

I had a friend, a peer, who was considering a new position and asked me what I thought. I asked if he had asked God what he should do. I told him that if he was being called to this job by God, he was assured success. If he was not being called, he was on his own. This is a critical point in the Christian walk. We need to be serving a higher purpose than our own. We must not think that our job is something that is ours and we go about it as if it is a parallel existence to our spiritual walk. Our walk is our existence, and our job is just something that we do while we are walking. Realizing this makes it easier to deal with day-to-day problems, frustrations, successes, and failures. Once you see your job as a way to honor God, you will see it and do it from a completely different perspective. Our flesh will never allow us to remove all stress and trust God fully, but much of the pressure can be relieved by trusting Him for your results. Clearly, I am not talking about going into work each day and sitting around doing nothing but repeating the mantra, "Go ahead and bless me Lord." That would certainly not bring any honor to God. But it is appropriate and scriptural to expect God to make your job go the way He wants if you are truly submitted to Him.

But what if things don't go well, and I don't get things done the way my company expects?

A tricky question indeed. It must start with the amount of faith you are exhibiting by trusting God to do your job for you and accepting the results He ordains according to His plan for your life. But what if things don't go well, and you get fussed at, maybe even fired? If you are submitted to accepting God's will, you should not be ashamed of doing your best and it not being enough for your employer. One reason we don't want to get fired is because it will hurt our pride. God may just want to remove you from your job because you are a bit too proud of it or your success in it. Maybe we are concerned about providing for our family. Once again, whom are we trusting for that provision, God or someone or something else?

Conditional Obedience

As I was growing in my walk, I once prayed to God that I would go anywhere and do anything He wanted me to do. I knew I could take anything the world can dish out, because if God is for me, who can be against me? I made a condition, however. I said, "Lord, just don't afflict my wife and children because I just couldn't handle that." I might as well have said, "Please smite me Lord." Putting your faith in the Father does not come with conditions.

You see, sometime after this moment, my wife was diagnosed with a benign brain tumor that had to be removed, and she was also later diagnosed with MS. My daughter ended up having heart surgery to correct a tachycardia condition. My son developed Tourette's Syndrome and had hip surgery when he was twenty years old. All are fine today, and their conditions are very mild, God be praised, but many would conclude that God treated me unfairly by allowing the very thing that I most feared in my life to become a reality. I don't see it that way at all. He taught me that He can bring me through anything, even that which I thought I could not handle.

This is important, because if you don't truly believe this, you will do your job as not to lose it rather than to glorify God in it, and your performance will be affected. It is equally important that not only did I learn that He will get me through anything, but I also learned that I must accept His judgment on my life. You can't get mad at God because things didn't turn out the way you wanted. Some say it's OK to get mad at God. I say, why would you? If you believe His will is perfect and His plan for your life is for your best, why would you question His result? I recall being grateful for these afflictions because I knew He was carrying me through all these trials, and I learned to trust Him more and more after each experience.

A God-Sized Thing

Very late in my career, a dear friend and brother in Christ approached me and told me about a new business he was going

to start. He had the product designed; a prototype was under
way, and a patent was pending. He asked if I would be interested in working for him and being the plant manager. He had
the business experience but was not a manufacturing guy, and
he knew I was. I immediately told him "No, I'm not interested," but because he was a friend, I said I would pray about
it. He responded with "That's all I can ask." I did pray about it
but had no intentions of leaving my current company with only
ten to twelve years to work before retirement. Even though I
had no intentions of joining him, I helped out by evaluating
some facilities he was considering for purchase to build the new
product. I made some estimates for startup costs and met with
his team to lay out the factory, just to help out. My wife and
daughter started encouraging me to take this opportunity. They
were worried about my health. I was nursing a heart condition
and had issues that landed me in the emergency room a couple
of times. My faith was strong, but my flesh was weak, and I still
fell prey to stress and a desire to be thought of as someone that
works hard and gets the job done.

My friend told me he couldn't match the salary of a major
corporation. I was still trying to provide for my family so this
was not an encouraging statement for him to make. You can
see from my discussion of family health crises how fond or
dependent we had become of good medical insurance; my
daughter had just finished private college, and my son was
just about to start private college with no scholarships. The
cost of my wife's MS medication without insurance was about
$11,000 a month. There was no way I could take this position
even if I wanted to. Oh how the natural man thinks.

*"But the natural man does not receive the things of the Spirit
of God, for they are foolishness to him; nor can he know them,
because they are spiritually discerned."* (1 Corinthians 2:14)

It was foolishness to even consider this opportunity—foolish for the natural man that is. I was intrigued by the shear lunacy of going to this position. I continued to pray. I considered all the reasons I could think of why God might want me to take this step.

Sometime later I was traveling on business and was asleep in a hotel room. It was 1:00 AM. I remember looking at the clock because I woke up with my eyes wide open. I began thinking about the position and got very excited about it. All the plans and possibilities started running through my mind. I had tremendous peace about the idea of leaving my current position. I clearly felt God calling me to do this thing. When I got home, I told my family, and they were very excited. This move made no sense, which made me even more convinced it was from God. I'm not saying that God is foolish, may it never be, but His ways are not our ways, and our ways are not His. I was suddenly excited about something I didn't want to do and was going to put me in bad financial shape. I wouldn't be able to provide great insurance for my wife and tuition, room and board for my son. I committed my fear to prayer and started figuring out what God was up to. He wanted me to trust Him for my family's provision and not my employer. This is easily said but difficult to do because we truly have to die to self and the idea that we provide all the things in our life when in reality, God provides all we have.

You may be thinking, *Wait a minute, I worked hard for everything I have. It wasn't given to me.*

I'm sure you did, and so did I, but you would not have your job and would not have the skill and work ethic to keep it had God not gifted you so.

My wife and I had been discussing how we wanted a "God-sized" thing to happen in our life. Well, this was it. We saw it as a "come to Jesus" season where we were going to have to let go of the side of the boat and trust Christ for everything, including doing the new job with a startup company. Wow! I could see how God had orchestrated my entire life for this season. How he gave me thirty years of experience in a field I never intended to enter so I could apply it in this place He wanted me and truly minister to people by providing jobs in a Christian environment complete with Bible studies (optional of course) and hiring practices that served people and God, not the almighty dollar. Yes, I could see it clearly; it was all coming together so I knew it had to be God's direction.

Only, it wasn't!

With the national recession that stifled business and lending in 2007, my friend could never get the financing he needed. He never started the new company and never went into production with the new product.

What was up with that?

Did I miss God?

Was all this spiritual stuff my own imagination?

Was God chastising me by putting me on this emotional roller coaster?

Why would God call me and not see it through?

Was this the test of Abraham, to see if I would put my security on the altar and follow Him?

Was God trying to teach me that I needed to depend only on Him?

Could it be that God is not working with me at all, but this is about my friend and what God wants to teach him?

How would I admit to my family and to others that knew about the opportunity that it wasn't going to happen?

Do I really know God's voice when I think I hear it?

Am I really not in fellowship enough to know His voice?

And here is the really dangerous assessment: *But I had it all figured out!*

That last assessment is dangerous first of all because it is a statement rather than a question. Secondly, because we can't "figure out" God. Remember, His ways are not our ways.

Just Do the Next Thing

At the end of this adventure, I was still asking these questions. Then came a Sunday School study about Elijah. I had studied and taught about Elijah before but had missed a fine detail. When God gave Him instructions, He did not lay out the entire plan for him. He just told him to go here or there. Then, when Elijah obeyed, God gave him new instructions. Again, not the entire plan, just the next thing. We should indeed be in fellowship with God to the point we hear His voice and know His will, but we shouldn't try to figure it out. He knows what He is doing, and if He lets us in on the entire plan, we wouldn't understand it and would therefore question it, or even worse, mess it up through our own intervention. A great way to get out ahead of God is to figure out where He is going and try to get there before Him, in our timing. So when you are approaching a God-sized calling on your life, do you want to venture ahead and be on your own or wait for Him and walk in His plan and under His protection? The answer is obvious.

But Randall, how do you do that without trying to figure out
where He is taking you? Isn't that part of knowing what to do
next?

I don't know. This is still a learning curve for me. When
I get the answer, I'll probably write another book on the subject. What I do know is that I don't have the answers to the
questions above, and I no longer care what the answers are.
I've stopped trying to figure it out. He told me to tell my
friend I would pray, and I did. He told me to prepare to take
the opportunity, and I did. He told me to trust Him for the
future, and I did. He then told me to stay at my job and fulfill
the ministry He has for me there, and I did, and was blessed
with numerous opportunities for ministry. At the time He was
preparing me for the new opportunity, He told me to do the
honorable thing and tell my boss I was leaving so he could
plan a backfill, and I did. My boss later told me, "I'm praying
against you on this because I need you here." Maybe that's
why the deal never went through, because God was honoring his request. "The prayers of a righteous man avails much."
Oops, there I go again, trying to figure it out. See how easy it is
to fall back into the habit. The "next thing" for me to do was
to minister to the people where I worked and glorify God by
the way I did my job and let God decide what the next "next
thing" would be. There is great peace in this.

The Company

It's difficult to talk about "the job" without considering "the
company." I find that many people have misconceptions about
the companies for which they work. I think it is a mistake to
personify the company, and it leads to errors in attitudes and
behaviors. The company is not a person; it is an entity. I man-

aged a group of people once that were having a lunchtime conversation. I walked in to overhear one say,

"This company doesn't care about me."

I replied, "You're right, it doesn't."

Jaws dropped, and eyes were fixed on me, anxious to hear an explanation. So, I gave them one.

"You're right, this company doesn't care about you, because it can't. The company can't care because it is not a person, it hasn't the ability to care. It exists for one reason only, to make more money this year than it made last year. People that work for the company have to do the caring."

We have to stop seeing the company for which we work as some big, bad bulldog that is just waiting to feed on our flesh. It is an entity that provides goods and services to the public in exchange for money. It is, however, led and directed by people who insert their moral, ethical, and intellectual DNA into the operation. This gives the company the appearance of a person but it's really the personality of employees that defines the personality of the company. This is important, because it helps us realize that our daily battles are not against an enemy called "the company"; it is against the business challenge that is before us. Once we realize this, it is easier to put away feelings such as "it's not fair," and "I should not be required to do this," or, "I'm not appreciated around here." Once we do this, we can begin to see our primary purpose at work is not to achieve fairness for ourselves, but to be on mission for God and His plan.

The Boss

And about that boss. Well, there is a way to show your witness by the way you react to your boss and those in authority over you. The Bible talks frequently about how a slave and a servant should act toward their master.

Wait a minute, I'm no slave or servant, and I have no master.

Of course, you're not, and you don't, but the teachings of the Bible that speak to this relationship can and should be applied to our work relationships because we are to be submissive to our earthly masters and obey their instructions. Submitting to authority is a step that must be taken before we can submit to God. If we cannot submit to the authority that has been placed over us in the workplace, we will never submit to the will of God. We must remember that no matter how unfair or undeserving our boss seems to be, God has placed that authority over us for His reasons and His purpose.

But you don't understand, my boss is a real skunk and doesn't deserve respect or obedience. Besides, respect must be earned, not just given.

Well, maybe you are not familiar with Romans 13:1–5:

"Let every soul be subject to the governing authorities. For there is no authority except from God, and the authorities that exist are appointed by God. Therefore, whoever resists the authority resists the ordinance of God, and those who resist will bring judgment on themselves. For rulers are not a terror to good works, but to evil. Do you want to be unafraid of the authority? Do what is good, and you will have praise from the same. For he is God's minister to you for good. But if you do evil, be afraid; for he does not bear the sword in vain; for he is God's minister, an avenger to execute wrath on him who practices evil. Therefore, you must be subject, not only because of wrath but also for conscience' sake."

This scripture refers to governments and rulers but can and should be applied to our bosses. While we're at it, we must also apply this to the government, maybe even more difficult to do. But as the scripture clearly explains, God has placed all authority over us for His purpose. If we are chastised, fussed at or disciplined, it may be in response to our evil, and God may be using them to be the minister of His justice. You may wonder what evil you have done. Maybe it is self-promotion, ambition, unjust actions against others, laziness, or animosity against the company or a person in the company. Maybe it is a more obvious evil such as embezzlement, stealing, sabotage, harassment or lying. You can easily see how God would use your boss to wield the sword of righteousness in these situations.

But what if your boss is evil, what should you do? How do you apply Romans 13?

I think you have to be careful not to do anything that is against God's ordinance even if you are directed to do so by your boss. If you find yourself in this situation, you should refrain from acting in a way that does not honor God or damages your witness for Christ, but at the same time you must be submissive. This means you must respectfully refuse, explore other ways to get the work done without acting in an evil manner, but accept the discipline that comes from not following the boss's directions. This may include termination, but you must be willing to accept this rather than going against God. If you stand for righteousness and still get disciplined or fired, you are under God's protection, and the judgment is against your boss. If you join your boss in evil, the judgment is against you as well as your boss. Accepting the consequences is what submission is about. It is trusting God for your provision and sustenance. Easy to write and read, much harder to do. It has something to do with picking up your cross every day.

But sometimes that boss is just not a solid citizen. You have to leave that situation between them and the Lord. You should try to reach them by showing them Christ in your life and not take it upon yourself to change or reform them. If God chooses to change them, He will use you as He wills to be the instrument of His revelation to your boss. Your role in this revelation is to intercede in prayer and be ready when called upon to give your witness of Jesus as your personal Lord and Savior.

The Evil Deep Inside You

Just as I mentioned earlier, your struggle is not against your boss, just as it is not against your company, it is against the evil that threatens your witness when you are tempted to disgrace the gospel of Christ with an unholy response to a work situation. Your boss is just an instrument that Satan will use to bring out the evil that exists inside you. I remember a wonderful object lesson I observed during a revival session (we cannot schedule revival, only revival meetings and sessions) led by Life Action Ministries. The leader took an orange, injected the center with ink and then cut a hole in the orange. As he squeezed the orange, he explained that it represented the pressure we experience in life. He showed how the clear, sweet orange juice began to come out as the pressure increased. The more pressure that is applied, the more of what is inside us comes out. Then he put extreme pressure on the orange, and the thing that was deep in the center came out, the black ink. This is just like our lives. We are pretty good under pressure for a while, and then all the good, clear, sweet stuff inside us comes out as we cope and/or react, but as the pressure increases the evil that is deep within us starts to come out. We all have our limits of how much we can take before the evil comes out, and the limit is different in everyone. Your boss is the same regardless if they are saved or not. We need to understand that they will have their limit as well, and if you see evil, it is the same that exists in all of us, they have just reached their limit. Knowing the Word of God and living your life as Jesus did will help raise your personal limit and also help you understand and forgive those that reach their limit much sooner than you.

CHAPTER

3

PERSPECTIVE

I am becoming increasingly intrigued by the concept of perspective. Everyone has their own, and not all perspectives are the same. Perspectives are formed over time and are based on life experience. Perspectives influence our perception and reaction to any situation. To truly communicate with someone, you must understand their perspective on a topic. If you don't, you are talking at someone and not to them. Communication is the attempt to present information to someone in a manner that they understand your position and why you hold it so. If your perspective is not taken into consideration, someone will disagree with you and start an argument with the purpose of changing your opinion or simply defending theirs, and you will respond in kind. At that point, communication has ceased, and competition has begun which demands a winner and a loser. I'm not saying that you have to agree with everyone or that you need to capitulate to another perspective. I'm just saying it is best to try to understand it because you will not be persuasive if you and someone are arguing two different subjects at the same time, which is what happens when two people don't recognize from where the other person is coming.

Perspective is the first step to persuasion, but persuasion can be the first step to a prideful fall. If we try too hard to get someone to understand our perspective, we can take on the challenge of persuading them to accept Christ. Sounds like a good thing, but remember my earlier comment that God calls and God saves. If we are not careful, we will take on the responsibility of someone accepting Christ and that is not our responsibility, it's theirs. We are to go and tell. If we forget this, we will engage in a verbal wrestling match that will eventually drive us to employ tactics that will have just the opposite impact because we will demonstrate the competitive, prideful attitude that seeks victory for one's self rather than the love of Christ that is offering eternal salvation. We would probably share more often if we didn't take on the pressure of convincing someone. That's not to say we shouldn't be persistent in sharing, even repeatedly to the same person, but we could become frustrated and impatient if we take on the responsibility to persuade. I think it is better to tell, explain, and disciple. The gospel itself has the power to persuade; our role is to tell.

It's important to articulate our perspective so that the person with whom we are sharing can understand where we are coming from and potentially understand our perspective. It is even more important to understand theirs because it will guide us in our approach to sharing. It is as simple as asking ourselves, *What will it take to get this person to understand what I am talking about?* It can also be an effective witnessing tool.

I was once in a conversation with an employee, a direct report, in my office where I had a Bible on my desk. The discussion was not about spirituality at all but she brought up the fact that she enjoys travel and wants to travel the world and learn about other cultures. She said that she wasn't a religious person but she likes to learn about people's beliefs and their perspectives. I launched into the interest I had in perspective and how it is critical to communication and learning. I gave the example that I was an evangelical Christian, which means my perspective is the Bible. I laid my hand on the Bible on my desk and said,

"You would never, ever convince me that the Bible is not the inspired Word of God, and you would never, ever change my mind about Jesus being the Son of God and that He died on the cross for my sin, and because I have accepted His sacrifice for the forgiveness of my sin I will have eternal life in heaven. Even though you would never convince me otherwise, I still enjoy hearing other beliefs and other perspectives."

In this way I was able to share the gospel and stay on the topic of discussion. She said she agreed totally, with the point about perspective anyway. She may not realize it now, but she had just been told the gospel message of Christ. Now it is up to her and the Holy Spirit as to what she does with it.

It is common for someone to approach me with a question about spiritual matters or about my advice on right and wrong. I always start my answer with my perspective.

"Well, you know I am an evangelical Christian, so my perspective is going to be from the Bible."

They generally accept that and respect it. Sometimes, they politely challenge the validity of the Bible. At this point you are no longer sharing your perspective but rather your defense of the faith. I used to limit my defense of the faith, to the statement,

"Hey, I didn't write it; I just believe it."

I have since taken more responsibility for the defense of my faith. I'm trying to prepare myself to give facts as well as beliefs to explain why I believe the Bible, but when it comes down to it, it's a matter of faith, as in do you have any or not?

Faith is really all you need to defend your beliefs. You may/will get challenged about your dedication to the Bible, which some do not believe is God's word at all and is full of inaccuracies and contradictions. Many will try to convince you that your belief is based on something that is not only without proof or foundation but is the practice and behavior of someone that is unintelligent, unenlightened, unscientific, superstitious, closed-minded, and is the source of all the problems in the world. You will experience people that give you all kinds of "scientific" arguments to contradict the Bible. Don't feel like you have to be able to counter their so called facts with facts of your own. Not everyone can be a Ph.D. seminarian that can "fence" successfully with any opponent. I'm certainly not, but I'm not intimidated, because if they get me into a position where I cannot counter their rhetoric, I just say,

"Well, it's what I believe; it's what I have faith in."

"But don't you agree with the facts I've given? Aren't you going to change your mind about the Bible?"

"No, because faith doesn't come from my mind, it comes from my heart. You are talking about agreeing with something you are calling fact and I'm talking about something that I am accepting by faith. They are two different things. Do you want to talk about facts, or faith?"

"I want to talk about facts."

"Oh, well, I don't know if what you've said is fact, and since it goes against my faith, I'm not ready to accept it as fact. Would you like to talk about faith?"

You see how perspective plays in? It's critical to bring clarity to the discussion in order to be on the same topic, even if you have to cut it short by saying "I don't know, but I can tell you what I believe."

"But how could you possibly believe that?"

"Because I know it to be true because of what I have experienced since I accepted Jesus as my Savior."

Now, this is something that an intelligent person should not argue. How could they possibly know better than you what you have experienced? Just keep the topic on faith and what it means to you and how it impacts your life.

Perspective Persuades

My wife is a brilliant communicator, if for no other reason, for the way she corrects my driving. She once said to me,

"You're driving like a maniac."

Of course, I was not, but that was her perspective. I responded with mine.

"No, I'm not, and how would you know? Have you ever driven with a maniac to know how one drives?"

You see, I could argue her perspective because she gave me an opportunity to do so. Not a response I recommend, by the way. The rest of the drive was quite lonely. So, being the brilliant communicator that she is, she learned to say,

"Your driving is scaring me and making me uncomfortable. Would you please slow down?"

What am I going to say?

Oh no it's not. You're not really scared, and you're not uncomfortable.

It would be quite stupid to make that remark, and she knew it. Her perspective was now something with which I could not argue. She won the point, and I slowed the car. This is an example of why perspective is important when sharing your faith and how it can be used as a tool. Remember, however, your task is not to win the point but to share the gospel.

There is also power in perspective. It's actually the power of God when sharing your faith, but some people will see your great conviction for your perspective and wish they could be as certain as you about what they believe. This might encourage them to seek more information about why you are so convicted. This is what you want to happen. If they are seeking and asking, you can answer their questions, even in the workplace. God's power will not be in the wind, nor the earthquake, nor in the fire, but in the still small voice (1 Kings 19:11-12).

In other words, show your conviction quietly as a teacher and friend, not as a conqueror or opponent. The more abrasive you are in sharing your perspective and faith, the more people will take offense and complain about you, which could possibly end your witness due to Human Resources reprimanding you and warning you not to discuss religion in the workplace.

Truth in Love

I hear a lot of preachers talk about sharing truth in love, but they turn right around and resort to name calling and degrading the sinner instead of the sin. This is not truth in love. May I share an example of what I consider to be the difference between sharing truth in love and sharing the truth without love?

I get asked from time to time,

"Are all Jews going to hell?"

Answering this without love would sound something like this:

"You bet your life they are. They don't believe in Jesus, and they crucified Him on the cross, so they are all hell-bound."

Telling the truth in love may sound more like this:

"I'm an evangelical Christian, a follower of Jesus Christ, so I believe what Jesus said in John 14:6, *"I am the way, the truth and the life. No man comes to the Father but through Me."* For that reason, I don't know how anyone, Jew, Muslim, Buddhist or anyone can go to heaven without accepting Jesus as Lord and Savior."

"But are they going to hell?"

"I don't know, that's between them and God, I just don't know of a way to heaven other than through Jesus."

Hopefully you see a difference. This difference will help you share your faith without offense. The gospel message is offense enough, so you really don't need to add to it. Don't be ashamed of the gospel, but don't be the offender as you share it.

By the way, I love the people of Israel and their Jewish heritage. The greatest vacation of my life was going to Israel, but I don't know how a person can enter heaven without accepting Jesus. I wish there were another way, I just can't find it in the Bible. I just shared two perspectives, loving God's chosen people and hoping for salvation for them but not putting that above what I know to be truth from scripture.

My son completed his Master of Letters degree from the University of St. Andrews in Scotland. His field of study is

Theology, Imagination, and the Arts. It is basically a study of how theology is expressed in various art forms. The requirements of his curriculum was to be able to defend his position regardless of his perspective, and he has become quite adept at this. We have had several theological discussions since his return, and I must admit I do not share his perspective on many things, but the point I would make is that we are able to discuss these things calmly because we spend much of the discussion clarifying our perspectives rather than arguing about two different things at the same time. I think I can relate to his perspective, even in disagreement, because he is "figuring things out" intellectually the same way I did as a young biology student. This allows me the discernment of the points I need to argue as inaccurate and which I need to describe as a matter of faith. This makes for a healthier conversation and exchange of ideas. This is particularly healthy, because we both agree on salvation by grace through faith in the blood of Jesus. Everything else is somewhat peripheral and need not be taken to the point of relationship-destroying arguments. After clarifying perspectives, I generally find his points to be valid, interesting, and worthy of consideration—without compromising the gospel of Christ.

Perspective and Preference
I have difficulty dealing with man's insistence that old-fashioned traditional worship is the only God-honoring way. If that were true, we would all worship in cathedrals and only sing Gregorian chants, or better still, meet in homes and sing praises in Hebrew, Aramaic, or Greek as the first church did.

I believe that worship comes from the heart and is something you should bring to the service, not something you get from the choir director or the pastor. That's why style of music, choice of instruments, no instruments at all, only singing verses 1, 2, and 4 from the hymnal, having the Lord's Supper weekly, monthly, or quarterly, whether to have announcements at the beginning or the end of service, and so forth, are all man-made preferences that are not ordained by God. These methods and observances are, however, a way to be organized in our worship to the point that there is not Sunday chaos without oversight of an elder, the pastor. He is responsible for what is said and taught in the service, so the floor should not be open to any theology that anyone would care to espouse were there no order of service. The pastor should also be open to the leading of the Holy Spirit and be willing to change the "order of service" on the fly if the Spirit so leads.

So, what does this have to do with perspective? I am giving examples of how my educated son and I are able to share varying ideas without argument or compromise through understanding each other's perspective. The words about "old time religion" is just one example of how one's perspective can interfere with sharing the gospel because if one is not careful, they will be sharing "religion" and their practice thereof rather than the gospel of Christ. Remember, the gospel message is grace through faith in the blood of Jesus; it is not "you must attend service on Sunday morning, Sunday night, and Wednesday night." This is important to understand, because people will use the practices of church as a reason to not accept Christ unto salvation. If your defense of the faith turns into a defense of your denomination or worship style, you are no longer sharing the gospel. There is nothing wrong with your preference for worship style, it's just critical that you realize it is human preference and not critical to the gospel message or one's faith in Jesus, so when someone gives the excuse,

"I knew someone once, and he did this and that at church, and I don't want to do that…"

You can explain that method is a church practice, but you would like to talk about accepting Christ as your Savior.

You should also be prepared for the perspective of the lost and how they do not want to give up some part of their life. I've heard from people,

"I like to go to the casino, and if I get saved, I would have to give that up",

or,

"I like to drink alcohol, and if I start going to church, I'd have to give that up",

or,

"I'm living with someone that is not my spouse, and if I do as you say, I would have to end that relationship."

If you feel confident in your ability as a Christian counselor, you can lead them out of that thinking, but if not, you can take that argument off the table. I usually tell people,

"Don't worry about that, just accept and be saved."

I take that approach for two reasons. One, because I know if they seek and accept, the Holy Spirit may soon lead them away from certain activities, and He is much better at that than I, and two, I'm concerned about the person with whom I am sharing getting the impression that you must be good enough and without sin before you can be saved. This is yet another example of how you can use perspective to make clear the free gift of salvation.

Perspectives often get clouded by terminology. Society has become such an identity-political, politically-correct, stereotyping, label-making existence that one can hardly exchange ideas without communication being cut off due to terminology. We have thrown away the dictionary and manufactured alternate meanings for so many words in the English language that one must continuously ask, "What do you mean by that?" or "How are you defining that?" I don't have many of these conversations because of my exposure to like-minded people for the most part, but when I do, I attempt to clarify a person's perspective and definition of the subject matter we are discussing. To be noncontroversial, I will use a nonsensical word, *fumumpt*. If someone asked, "Are you a fumumpt?" I would say, "That depends; what is your definition of a fumumpt?" The way they define the word will give you their perspective on the subject. Once they define it, you can answer according to their perspective, and then communication happens. Let's say that my working definition of a *fumumpt* is someone that likes *fums* but hates *umpts*. When asked, the person to whom you are speaking defines it as someone that hates *fums* and *umpts*. You actually like *fums* and do not like *umpts* so by your definition, your answer would be "yes." By their definition (perspective) you would have to answer "no."

You're probably thinking, *OK, Randall, you totally lost me on the fumumpt thing.*

Well, just substitute that word with one of your choosing, and it may be clearer. Here is a short list of examples that I find requires definition before discussing:

Calvinist, Armenian, dispensationalist, greenie, woke, conservative, liberal, moderate, racist, imperialist, born-again, saved, redneck, progressive, PC, nationalist, globalist.

This is in no way an exhaustive list, but you get the idea. I wouldn't want to discuss these topics without knowing how the other person defines these terms when used. If you do not clarify, you may be discussing/arguing two different perspectives at the same time.

This is critical when sharing your faith. It could be as simple as:

"Are you saved?"

"Yes, I go to church sometimes. I think it's a good thing to do."

"Oh, OK, good."

Not the answer you were seeking and not what you needed to know.

My current perspective is that I have written enough about perspective. I hope you get the point. Perspective is a major consideration when sharing your faith, whether on the job or in the community.

4

ALWAYS BE READY TO GIVE A DEFENSE

"*But sanctify the Lord God in your hearts, and always be ready to give a defense to everyone who asks you a reason for the hope that is in you with meekness and fear; having a good conscience, that when they defame you as evildoers, those who revile your good conduct in Christ may be ashamed.*" (1 Peter 3:15–16)

Let me first reiterate that it is critical to understand that when you share your faith, especially in the workplace, you will be challenged, and so will your beliefs, but it is not imperative that you be able to answer any theological question that someone may throw at you. You are armed with the gospel of Jesus Christ, and the Holy Spirit is in you, instructing you what to say. If you share the gospel of Christ crucified, you have done what you are called to do. Remember, you cannot save anyone; only God can. We are, however, called to be able to give a defense for what we believe, as Peter said. The deeper you go into the Bible and submit yourself to sound teaching, the more desire and ability you will have to tell others why and how you believe as you do. This is called *apologetics*, the defense of the faith. I had a friend once tell me he didn't like that term, and I can relate, because I once felt the same.

I didn't feel I had to apologize for believing the way I did. I obviously didn't understand the meaning of the term. It's not apologizing, it's giving a defense for your faith.

Our society today is not looking for a reason to believe, but rather a reason not to believe. That is why the challenges come so easily and frequently. The world demands proof. I shared the gospel once with a coworker, and after talking for an hour, the thing that impressed him the most was when I said my responsibility was not to prove Jesus; I just had to tell about Him. I told him it was up to him what he did with it now that he had heard the gospel. So, for those that are full of the Word and want to share it as Peter encouraged, here are some discussions I've had or heard that may help you in your apologetics.

Seekers

Let's start with those that are truly seeking. They have questions, and they are curious about the hope you have. Hope that is strong enough to influence you into a life that is different than most. They may be desperate because they cannot seem to make their lives turn out the way they want, or even worse, they cannot make their lives even livable. They are living life without hope. They may have experienced marital troubles, broken relationships, trouble with children, financial disaster, illness, or maybe even a loss through death that they cannot get beyond due to a lack of understanding, acceptance, or a sense of justice. So many people live in misery because they cannot receive recompense or retribution for something bad that's happened in their life. They are so angry with God that the only way they know to get their pound of flesh is to reject Him until He proves Himself worthy to them.

Let's begin with that question.

How can you believe in a god that you say is loving but allows such bad things to happen to people?

First of all, the question is correct in saying that God *allows*, but He doesn't always *cause* bad things to happen, He rather allows the free choice of man to dictate what happens. God didn't create sin, disease, and death. He made man perfect, without those things, but man's choice brought those things into the world. Yes, God cursed Adam, Eve, and the entire world, but that was a consequence of their sin, their disobedience. Disease, death, and tragedy in the world today are consequences of man's free choice. We are free to choose what we will do or believe but there will be consequences, and the consequences of our sin may affect others. Like the drunk driver that takes out a family that was not sinning at the time of the accident.

But why doesn't He stop innocent people from getting hurt or sick?

Who is innocent?

Jesus said: *"Why do you call me good? None are good but One: that is God."* (Matthew 19:17)

Paul wrote to the Romans: *"For all have sinned and come short of the glory of God."* (Romans 3:23)

The consequence of a world fallen in sin is bad things happen, and no one is innocent. Rather than blame God when bad things happen, we should praise Him when they do not.

I just can't believe that a loving God would condemn anyone to hell.

First of all, God does not condemn anyone to hell, they condemn themselves.

"For God so loved the world that He gave His only begotten Son, that whoever believes in Him should not perish but have

*everlasting life. For God did not send His Son into the world
to condemn the world, but that the world through Him might
be saved. He who believes in Him is not condemned; but he
who does not believe is condemned already, because he has not
believed in the name of the only begotten Son of God. And this is
the condemnation, that light has come into the world, and men
loved darkness rather than light, because their deeds were evil.
For everyone practicing evil hates the light and does not come to
the light, lest his deeds should be exposed."* (John 3:16–20)

Imagine you had a child, and his/her life was required to
pay for someone's wrongdoing, and it was your child's idea to
give their life for someone else, and they told you they didn't
do anything wrong but if giving their life would keep the
wrongdoer from suffering the consequences of their actions
they would willingly do it because they wouldn't want anyone to experience those consequences. So, they do it, give their
lives, and the wrongdoer goes free without consequence. Then,
the wrongdoer wants to suffer the consequences anyway, and
you explain that they should not because your child paid the
debt in full and won their freedom. The wrongdoer then says
that your child's life was not sufficient, and they do not accept
that payment, and they experience the consequences anyway.

You would likely be thinking, *What? My child was innocent
and gave their life so you could continue yours and you're now saying
it's not enough and that my child sacrificed their life for nothing?*

I'm sure your wrath would burn against the wrongdoer,
and you would be willing to see them receive the consequences
of refusing to accept your child's sacrifice. Is this not the sce-
nario with God?

God gives all a choice and a way to salvation and is longsuffering with those that have not accepted.

"The Lord is not slack concerning His promise, as some count slackness, but is longsuffering toward us, not willing that any should perish but that all should come to repentance." (2 Peter 3:9)

So, if God is willing for all to repent, why doesn't He save everyone?

God allows some to remain lost so He can rejoice more in those that are saved.

"Does not the potter have the power over the clay, from the same lump to make one vessel for honor and another for dishonor? What if God, wanting to show His wrath and to make His power known, endured with much longsuffering the vessels of wrath prepared for destruction, and that He might make known the riches of His glory on the vessels of mercy which He had prepared beforehand for glory." (Romans 9:21–23)

There is no light without the contrast of darkness. There is no good without the contrast of evil. God takes greater pleasure in the saved, knowing that not all will choose to accept.

Why do Christians think Jesus is the only way to heaven? This can't be true, because there are billions of people that don't believe in Jesus as their savior, and surely that many people will not go to hell.

Jesus says in John 14:6: *"I am the Way, the Truth and the Life. No man comes to the Father except through Me."*

This excludes there being many ways to heaven. As far as there being billions of people that spend eternity in hell, Jesus also says in Matthew 7:14: *"Because narrow is the gate and difficult is the way which leads to life, and there are few who find it."*

Those people who think God would not allow billions of people to go to hell are not followers of Jesus Christ, even though they claim to be Christians, and they are creating God in their own image.

Well, I wouldn't believe in or serve a god that would send people to hell.

Then you've made your choice, and I beg and pray you will change your heart and mind.

Other Excuses

I don't go to church, there's nothing but hypocrites there.

That's true, there are hypocrites and even worse. There are liars, thieves, adulterers, pornographers, child molesters, murderers, blasphemers, bigots, cheats, drug addicts, and swindlers. I had a pastor once say that church is not a hotel for saints but rather a hospital for sinners. The people in church are no better than the people that neither believe nor attend, but they are different. Most, but not all, are saved. They are "justified" before God and are at church to learn to be "sanctified" before Him as well. Being "justified" means your sins are forgiven. Being "sanctified" is a process by which you are transforming to the image of Christ and learning to live like Him. It's important to admit that not everyone in church is saved. As my wife says, being in church doesn't make you a Christian any more than being in a garage makes you a car (not an original of hers, and I don't know who originally said it). I was raised in church without being saved for twenty-five years. Then I accepted that my good works and deeds would not atone for my sins and get me into heaven; only the blood of Jesus could do that.

I think it's a good idea to tell the person who gives this church argument that they are talking about church and you would like to talk about salvation. Church is a great place to go to worship God for what He has done for you and learn about His promises and how to live life abundantly in Him. If the person still has doubts, tell them that church is a place to learn about Jesus' sacrifice on the cross and how accepting that can lead to eternal life. You should encourage the person to not confuse salvation with church and explain the difference as I have above.

But if I get saved, I will have to give up things in my life that I really enjoy doing.

I tell people not to worry about giving things up, just accept Jesus' blood for the forgiveness of your sins.

You mean my sins are forgiven even if I continue doing them?

Yes. Christ died for the forgiveness of all sins, past, present, and future. You must repent of these sins or be judged by them in eternity, but at least it will be an eternity in heaven if you just receive. Again, I take this approach because I want to get their focus off being good enough and onto salvation being a free gift of God. Jesus does not want us to clean up our lives in order to be saved; He wants us to be saved in order to clean up our lives and live it abundantly without the guilt of sin. I said "guilt," not conviction. The Holy Spirit will still convict us of our sin, and if a person does not repent (turn back) from continuously practicing something they know is sinful, one would have to wonder if their salvation is genuine.

"But God demonstrates His own love toward us, in that while we were still sinners, Christ died for us." (Romans 5:8)

Preachers are negative, always talking about the evil of sin, and I don't want to go to church and be fussed at for an hour and be reminded how bad I am.

That's true, many preachers talk about the evil of sin, at least the good ones do. If you don't know the depth of your sin, how will you understand your need for a savior? If you don't understand your need for a savior, how can you ever truly accept Jesus as your Savior from sin unto salvation? There is a growing trend in our country of preachers and ministries that like to focus on the positive promises of God and neglect the negativity of sin and its consequences in our lives. Some of these ministries grow by the thousands because people feel good about a positive message stemming from God's positive promises. These preachers are doing a disservice to their congregants because the promises of God only apply to His children, those who have accepted Christ as Savior.

All churches have people in attendance that are there to hear a positive message. They want to "cash-in" on God's promise for an abundant life. If this were the only message God wanted His children to hear, then why is the Bible, and the New Testament in particular, full of descriptions of sin and our need for being "saved" from it? Matthew, Mark, Luke, and John were inspired by God to write about what Jesus said about sin in the Gospels, and Paul was certainly inspired to write about sin that was prevalent in the church in his epistles. I consider this to be compelling, that preachers should teach their flocks about sin, but then reiterate the gospel, the Good News that no matter how deep our sin, greater still is God's grace that saves us from it through Christ's blood on the cross, and through it, we can have abundant life. This means abundant life through spiritual contentment, joy, and peace, not abundant wealth and material prosperity. Continual preaching of a sinless, positive message is rebuked in the Bible as "tickling the ears," telling people what they want to hear but denying them the truth.

"Preach the word! Be ready in season and out of season. Convince, rebuke, exhort, with all longsuffering and teaching. For the time will come when they will not endure sound doctrine, but according to their own desires, because they have itching ears, they will heap up for themselves teachers; and they will turn their ears away from the truth, and be turned aside to fables." (2 Timothy 4:2–4)

I just don't want to give up control of my life to anyone or anything.

Well, that could be a problem. One of the costs of eternal salvation is making Jesus the Lord of your life. This means surrendering your life to Him and allowing Him through the guidance of the Holy Spirit to lead you through life according to His will. This is a process of surrender and not a momentary submission. As you become convinced that Jesus can do a better job running your life than you can, you will want to surrender more and more to Him, but it is still a slow and progressive surrender. I once heard Brad Stein, a Christian comedian, say how he hates to see the bumper sticker that says, "God is my copilot." He says that if the Creator of the universe is in the car with you, LET HIM DRIVE! This is good advice for those who do not want to give up control of their lives.

I don't trust this as the true way. What if there is something else I must do and I don't do it? I don't want to go to hell.

How will you ever know that any way you find is the right way? At least the Way of Jesus is documented and has been around for thousands of years. In His way, all you have to do is believe and accept. What could be easier or simpler? Any other way would just be man's invention based on what they "feel" is right.

"There is a way that seems right to a man, but its end is the way of death." (Proverbs 14:12)

"Trust in the Lord with all your heart, and lean not on your own understanding; in all your ways acknowledge Him, and He shall direct your paths." (Proverbs 3:5–6)

There will be times when you will answer these arguments with sound, biblical responses, but the person still refuses to accept Christ. Maybe it's time for some hardline closers and time to stop treating it as an intellectual challenge and give it over to the Holy Spirit as a spiritual battle and let Him fight it. A couple of closers might be:

"What do you have to lose if you accept? If I'm wrong, and you accept, you will live a life that offers peace, having faith in your eternal destiny. When you die, you'll end up in the same place you would have been if you had not accepted but you will have lived in peace. If I'm right, and you accept, you gain the peace in this life and everlasting life in glory."

An even harder line you can take is scriptural.

"I know you are searching for the truth. The Bible says: 'For the wages of sin is death....' You must decide if the wages will be paid by your death, or Christ's."

Dissenter

These are some ideas of how to answer the questions of someone that is searching. What about the person who is not—a true dissenter? This is a more difficult situation because they must be approached in a different manner, and with much more caution. Where the seeking person will most likely initiate the conversation, the dissenter will most likely not because they are not at all interested, and if they are, they may just want to pick a fight. If you approach a dissenter without invitation you run a very real risk of harassment charges, so you must be willing to submit to the consequences. I will later offer suggestions on how to do it with minimum risk.

First, let's look at different types of people who are not interested in spiritual things, the non-seekers. They are people who are ignorant of spiritual things. They were not raised in church; they have not been exposed to theology or the Bible. They know that some people think there is a God, heaven, and hell, but they don't realize they even have a soul that is at risk. Because of their attitude, they are totally tuned out and disinterested in the topic. Let's call them Group 1 people.

Group 2 people would be those who believe there is a God yet develop their own ideas of what He thinks is right and wrong and then live by that self-composed moral code. Because they make up the code, they are comfortable in it and see no need to learn about the Bible or deepen their relationship with God, let alone have a need for a savior.

Group 3 people are those that are only convinced by those things their intellect can process to the point of understanding. They "think" of everything but don't "believe" in anything. If they have anything resembling a god, it's science and reason.

Group 4 people are much like those in Group 3 but much more dangerous. Not only do they not believe but they take intellectual offense in anyone that does believe. Some make it part of their social calling to "enlighten" and save the world from any religious beliefs or practices. They are openly antagonistic toward religious people, especially Christians, and are usually more than ready to start or join a verbal argument to voice and spread their perceived enlightenment.

Let's look at some different approaches that can be used with each of these groups.

Group 1:

These are people who have no religious background or teaching and no knowledge of possessing a soul that has an eternal status. They know that some people believe in and follow a supreme being whom they call God, but they have no interest in finding out more about Him or changing their lives to follow His commands. They don't care if you believe; it just doesn't apply to them, and they have no desire to try to apply this "belief system."

One approach you might take is to show them the love of Christ. Remember, they are unaware of the need of God or a savior. If you are intentionally kind to them, they may ask why, why are you like that? You may want to demonstrate exceptional forgiveness in their presence, forgiveness of them or someone they have observed doing you wrong. This may prompt them to ask you why you do that. You can explain that Christ forgave you and that you are compelled to forgive others. Be prepared for someone to ask how He forgave you. That's when you need to be ready to present the gospel in full. It's important to do it calmly, without judgmental tones and without comparing yourself to them or any other person. You should explain what a good deal it is for you to be saved and see if they will become curious enough to ask for more information. It can sometimes be effective to answer questions as asked and give the impression that you are willing to share but not trying to preach at them or convince them your way is the only correct way to live. If they stop asking questions or show no interest, you may want to ask,

"Are you interested in learning about Christianity?"
Or…
"Do you know much about Christianity?"

If they say they are not interested in learning about Christianity, you may want to guide the conversation this way.

"Are you not interested because you know something about it and disapprove, or do you just not have any interest in spiritual things?"

If they respond with something like, "I know about Christianity and I disapprove," then you can reply with, "Can you be more specific of what you disapprove?"

You can then clear up any misinformation they may have. If they respond with no interest in spiritual things, you may challenge them in this manner.

"Do you believe you have a soul?"

"Yes, but I think it is of my own making, the way I choose to live my life."

You can then explain that God gives them their soul and spirit, and it is He that commands it. Then tell them what you know to be true about God.

"But I don't believe in God."

"Oh, but I do. Can I share with you why I believe?"

If they say yes, explain. If they say no, ask if you can share with them the gospel of Jesus.

If yes, then do so. If no, perhaps you can say something like…

"I believe Jesus is coming back soon, and, even if He doesn't, I would hate to think you would die someday without ever hearing the gospel."

"Well, I don't believe that."

"I understand, but I will go to heaven when I die, or when Jesus returns because I have accepted God's free gift of salvation through Jesus' death on the cross to redeem my sins, and

I hope I will see you there someday because you have done the same."

In saying this, you have shared the gospel with them. The rest is up to them and God.

If they say that they don't know much about Christianity, start with the gospel.

Group 2:

These are people who say they believe in God but don't need to improve their relationship with Him. If you can get them into a discussion, they will probably give you many statements about Him that are not biblically accurate, because they don't know or believe what the Bible says about God and are making up how they think God should be. Since these people are making up what they believe about God, you should challenge the origin of their belief.

"I believe God is good, loving and would never send anyone to hell."

"What is your basis for believing that about God?"

"I don't know, I just think that's what God is like."

"I think you mean that's what you would like God to be like. You really don't believe there is a God, do you?"

"Why, of course I do."

"If He is the Supreme Being of the universe, why do you think you can make up what He is like. Don't you think He is what He is and we are to learn about that rather than make up what we want Him to be?"

"Well, why do you think you know what He is like?"

"Because I have the Bible that tells me what He is like, what He loves and what He hates."

"I don't believe the Bible is inspired by God, it is just a book of stories from men."

"Then you have no foundation for what you believe and are, therefore, making it up. And if you don't believe in the Word, I don't know how you can believe in Jesus."

John 1:1 says, *"In the beginning was the Word, and the Word was with God and the Word was God."*

"That Word is Jesus. If you don't believe the Word, how can you believe in Jesus? The Bible needs to be the foundation of your belief. Your foundation needs to start with the gospel."

You should then share it with them. This may show them they need to continue their spiritual walk that includes learning more about what the Bible says about God and how He wants us to worship Him and live our lives. I had a friend once say to me that we all worship and serve God in our own way. I told him that as I go through life, I try to learn how to worship and serve the way He wants, in His way.

"Well, who are you to say that I'm making my religion up and I'm not worshiping the way God wants?"

"I'm saying that you can't identify the basis for your belief in God, so how could you know how to worship Him in the manner He requires? How can you know about salvation? Are you sure of your salvation?"

"I don't need salvation, I just have to live a good life and do more good than bad, and I will go to heaven."

"How do you know you've done more good than bad? Are you keeping score? Are you sure you know what God considers good and bad? Are you sure you are going to heaven when you die?"

"I guess I won't know until I get there."

"But you can know for sure."

At this point you can share the gospel in full.

Group 3:

This is the group who typically serves science and intellect as their god. They will only accept and believe in what they can "figure out" and explain. Their spiritual walk does not involve seeking God and developing a deeper relationship with Him but rather a journey of learning, explaining, reasoning and most importantly, proving. Since they have no true relationship with God, they cannot prove Him. He does not prove Himself to them because they cannot hear His calling or His leading through the Holy Spirit, because their spirit is not teachable. They rely only on what they can see, touch, smell, taste or imagine. They limit their perceptions to that which they can explain by earthly and carnal means.

Jesus told Thomas in John 20:29: *"Thomas, because you have seen Me, you have believed. Blessed are those who have not seen and yet have believed."*

There are some that even profess to believe in God—but on their terms. They explain Him as some form of energy that can be captured, manipulated, and forced to obey the commands of science. To them, He is limited to powers afforded Him by the textbooks of libraries and universities.

Some take a more philosophical approach. God is love; God is what is good in people; God is that which brings peace into our lives. All of these things are attributes of God, but He is so much more. How arrogant is it that any human can claim to possess the ability to describe Him!

Most, however, will try to argue the existence of God. Some may even seek to insult your intellect because you would believe in such a superstitious concept. You would have to deliver proof for them to entertain the thought at all. I usually tell these folks that God has proven Himself to me and that's all the proof I need. They typically come back with something to the effect of there being no scientific proof for God.

I ask them,

"How can the thing which is created be used to define that which created it?"

"What? That makes no sense!"

"Of course, it does. God created the universe and all that is within it. Being the Creator, He is far above anything that He has created, including the laws of science. Being the Creator, He does not have to follow the rules of the things He created such as the laws of science. So, why would you expect Him to prove himself in that way? Why would you expect science to be able to explain and define Him when He is the one who defined science? No, I don't think it is something you will ever prove or disprove, it's something you accept in faith. Yes, it's about faith in something you cannot prove by physical means. If you believe and receive Him, He will no doubt prove Himself to you."

If they still go hardline with you, you may have to go hardline back with them.

"Well, I just don't believe in things I cannot prove."

"I understand, and that is your choice to make. I just encourage you to make the choice that will allow you to have everlasting life. You know, I bet there are a lot of things you believe in but cannot prove."

"Like what?"

"Well, do you believe the Earth orbits the sun and the moon orbits the Earth?

"Yes, of course.

"But you can't prove it."

"Yes, I can because it happens every day and I can see it."

"True, you see it come and go every day but you don't know that it orbits."

"Well, scientists have proven it and that's enough for me."

"No, they have not proven it to you, they've told you and you've chosen to believe it. In the same way, Jesus and the writers of the Bible told me, and I've chosen to believe them. Do you believe there was a Babylonian empire?"

"Yes."

"Why?"

"Because there are ancient writings and archeological relics that describe it."

"I agree and believe there was a Babylon for the same reason as you. But I also believe the ancient writings of the Bible as the same proof as that offered by archeologists about Babylon. By the way, Babylon is mentioned in the Bible."

At this point, you may have to let the Holy Spirit take over and do the convincing. The key here is to remain calm, non-condemning and to be reasonable so they may think about what you've said and come back later for more discussion.

Science

As for science, it is based on theories of reason. Some, not all, can be proven and repeated in a laboratory. Science could not hope to prove or disprove God for the forementioned reasons. Science spends its resources trying to disprove God by offering alternatives as to how things come about without the existence of a supreme being. Take the theories of evolution, and by the way, there is no "theory" of evolution but rather many "theories," some of which scientists do not all agree are accurate. These theories combine to support an intellectual approach that all life started as a lower organism and evolved into what we see today due to environmental stress. Darwin himself had doubts about his theories because he could not find the fossil record to support an unbroken chain of progression in organismal evolution.

I agree that organisms change as a result of environmental stress. Unlike most Christians, I even agree that organisms can adapt and change to the point that they become a new species, but that doesn't prove there is no God. All animal life is made up of proteins, which are made up of amino acids, which are made up of carbon, nitrogen, hydrogen, and oxygen, which is made up of protons, electrons, and neutrons.

"But Professor, where did the electrons come from?"

"Oh, they just always were."

To me, this takes more faith than believing in God that created all. You could never prove that the smallest element of life, let's say electrons, just "always were." It is intellectually staggering to think there is such a thing as reverse eternity and that things had no beginning, no creation, and certainly no proof. One would have to accept that on faith.

I'm not anti-science. God has used science and scientists to bring about wonderful things for mankind. In fact, I am a scientist by education, just not by vocation. Because of my scientific training, I also know there is some shoddy science out there. Deductive reasoning is a gift not all scientists possess, which leads to unproven conclusions. I love the joke about the science study that measured the distance a frog could jump after his arms and legs were removed. The scientist would shout "jump" at the frog and measure the distance the frog covered in its leap. The distance would naturally become shorter with each arm or leg that was removed. Once all were removed, the frog covered no distance after several shouts. Conclusion: After removing all arms and legs, the frog becomes deaf. This joke is not very funny, but it demonstrates how scientists can take facts and misinterpret them to draw a false conclusion.

You may want to use some of these discussion points when sharing your faith with a Group 3 person. Remember to present your perspective but not get into a heated argument that would hurt your witness. If you don't feel confident discussing science, you may want to go back to...

"I don't know about that. All I know is there was a man. His name was Jesus..."

Group 4

I say that this group is dangerous because if someone is going to complain and get you in trouble for sharing your faith, it's them. They take intellectual and legal offense to anyone who believes in God and will be on mission to prevent religious propagation in the workplace, the community, in society or the world. Some are innocently acting on their own opinions, but others could be a tool of Satan. We should realize that possibility when we confront them because that puts us not only in an intellectual battle but a spiritual one as well. You need to be prayed up and prepared for this group if you are going to take them on.

Remember, "...because He that is in you is greater than he that is in the world." (1 John 4:4)

If you follow the advice from the early chapters, you have a right to share when people ask why you are different, and the

Group 4 people do not have a leg to stand on if they object. If we are about spreading the gospel, as we should be, that means sharing it with the Group 4 people as well. When they object to your sharing, you may want to try something like this:

"You seem to disagree and object to my beliefs."

"I do indeed."

"Do you know enough about what I believe to be able to disagree and object?"

"Yes, I know you believe in a god that created all and rules overall, and I can't agree with that or the fact you are telling others about this nonsense."

"Do you tell others that you believe there is no God?"

"Yes!"

"Why do you think you should be able to tell what you believe and I should not be allowed to tell what I believe?"

"Because what you believe is wrong."

"That's your opinion and perspective, but I think I should be allowed to have mine, and before you judge it, you should know what my perspective is. You are correct in saying I believe in God, the Creator and Ruler of all things, but I also believe He sent His son Jesus to die on the cross for my sins that they may be forgiven and that I can live forever in heaven if I just accept that and depend on no other means to secure my salvation."

In doing this you have shared the gospel with them in the context of a conversation rather than a proselytizing threat. The rest is up to the Holy Spirit because this person is not likely to want to continue the conversation other than to argue your position.

"I know that's what you believe, and I think that's !@#$%$%."

"I understand, but I wanted to make sure you were knowledgeable of what you were disagreeing with. I will make myself available if you want to discuss it further."

At this point you have done your job; you have shared the gospel. If they come back to discuss later, it is by their volition, and you can continue to share as you see fit because they asked for the information. They will most likely want to do so to discredit your belief and satisfy their own pride of intellect. Remember, they are on mission as well. If they do attempt to discredit your belief, it is best to stick to the gospel and the fact you are accepting these things by faith and not let them trap you into some argument that puts you in a position that you may say something they can use to end your witness to others. When you are dealing with a Group 4 person, you must have faith the Holy Spirit will convict as God sees fit and that you are there to plant the seed of the gospel. You will most likely have to follow the advice Jesus gave to the apostles when he sent them out to spread the Good News.

"And whoever will not receive you nor hear your words, when you depart from that house or city, shake the dust from your feet." (Matthew 10:14)

This was symbolic to those that would not receive the gospel. It was to be "a testimony against them" as Mark 6:11 puts it, but it was also a command that if the house or city would not have any part of the gospel from the apostles, then the apostles were to have no part of the house or city, not even the dust from the ground. They were to leave it behind. At some point you must also take the advice Jesus gave about continuing to strive with a Group 4 person who seeks to destroy the Gospel message.

"Do not give what is holy to the dogs; nor cast your pearls before swine, lest they trample them under their feet, and turn and tear you in pieces." (Matthew 7:6)

It's hard to come to this point if you truly have a burden for the lost, but you should examine your heart to see if this is a burden or a prideful contest to win the argument.

Jesus says in Matthew 12:30: *"He who is not with Me is against Me, and he who does not gather with Me scatters abroad."*

The Group 4 person is not only not with Christ, but is trying to scatter people abroad by keeping them from accepting. They are hurting the cause of Christ and can rightfully be considered "dogs" and "swine" as Jesus referred. If you involve yourself in vain arguments you give the Group 4 person more ammunition to discredit the witness of Christ. Conversely, if you deliver the gospel message in an honorable and loving way without hatred, anger, or compromise, you may just win over the person.

These are a few ideas you may want to consider when witnessing to people who are not seeking a relationship with God. It is certainly not an exhaustive list, but may help you develop similar approaches as you encounter such people. In short, be respectful and loving but do so as someone that is not ashamed of the Gospel of Christ. Do not compromise or apologize.

CHAPTER

5

THREE-STAGE PEOPLE

S o, we've discussed the type of people you may encounter as you attempt to share your faith in the workplace, but there is still another that must be approached cautiously. I have chosen to approach the writing in this chapter delicately, because I do not want to present the appearance of being judgmental, which could distract readers. The group I'm referring to is a group of Christians that are very well-meaning, devout, and zealous for the gospel. People that are trying to stand for God's righteousness. So, why would I ever be concerned about such people? It sounds like they've got it going on with Jesus and should be what all of us are striving to be. In some ways they are just that, but in others they can be an obstacle in the sharing of your faith. I will refer to these folks as Second Stage people.

To describe these good people, I must first discuss a theory, an observation I've made over thirty-seven years of walking with the Lord. I have observed in every person to which I have had the privilege to witness their entire walk, from salvation to semi-maturity, that there are three distinct stages that every Christian passes through in their road to spiritual maturity. Some Christians get caught in one of the stages and never make it to the next, but most make it out of Stage One only to spend a long time in Stage Two. A few, but very few, move rapidly to Stage Three and are truly guided by the Holy Spirit and are called to a special purpose. If you recognize a Stage Three person, you should hitch your plow to their tractor and allow them to pull you through your walk while turning up the soil of the hearts of people and readying them to receive the seeds of the gospel. They will be the most effective. The farming metaphor is figurative of course, but hopefully you can see through the poetry to understand of which I speak.

So, what are these imaginary stages that seemingly only I have noticed? I've never read a theologian that acknowledged these stages or heard a preacher espouse their existence. I'm not special, just observant. In addition, I passed through two stages myself, so I am intimately aware of their existence. You may have noticed them yourself and are already prepared to discern these stages in Christians you meet and are on guard to prevent them from distracting or injuring your witness, and if such is the case, I say, "Cool!", as you are indeed blessed. I should think that most are not aware of these stages and would never recognize them as something that could interfere with their witness, so I decided to write about them.

Stage One
Have you ever noticed a person when they first come to salvation? It is typical, not in every case, but typical, that the person has truly been changed by the saving grace of Jesus Christ and is on fire for the Lord. They spend a great deal of time in the Bible and are at church every time the door is open. They tend to hunger for service to the body and volunteer for many needs in the church. They spend a great deal of time talking to

the pastor and others to ask questions about interpretations of scripture, and they generally attend as many Bible studies as they can. They start listening to Christian music on the radio. They immediately change many things about their lives, but not everything. You can see evidence of the Holy Spirit speaking to their souls and beginning to lead their lives. Because they are new Christians, they are not sure of their faith other than that which brought them to salvation. They tend to want to live by God's Word but really don't understand what it says yet. They may have been raised in church and heard sermon after sermon but have not heard many under the influence of the Holy Spirit—and therefore have not taken in God's true meaning. They want so much to understand and be a part of the "inner sanctum" of Christianity that they start quoting and misquoting scripture, many times missing the context completely.

Perhaps, you're thinking, *But Randall, why is this a bad thing?*

It's not. In fact, it's a beautiful thing to see someone come to salvation and the many changes it brings to the lives of a new creature. It's a stage and a process that we all must go through. The only danger is when a person never makes it out of this stage. But what does that look like? Let's complete the list of characteristics, then discuss the "so what" of it all.

I once knew a man who attended the same church as I, and we spent a couple of years in a men's group together. This man was in his twenties, recently married, and a new Christian. Let's call him Bo. Bo had a comfortable life growing up, and his new wife was from a wealthy family. Like many privileged young people, they put a priority on entertainment. They were pretty heavy into drugs and alcohol. Bo would come to the men's group and give an update on his attempted sobriety. Most weeks he did very well, and it was obvious that Christ was making a difference in his life and in his wife's.

Some mornings he would report a fall that usually initiated an argument with his wife. She was trying to clean up as well but would smoke pot and bring a reprimand from Bo. This would start a fight, and Bo was unable to cope, so he would take comfort in intoxication either through pot or alcohol. This would take place even after they had children. I thought it odd that he would have falls such as this but then would tell stories how he shared Christ with people at work, perfect strangers. He seemed to be much bolder than I, and I was so impressed, dare I say convicted, by his passion for sharing Christ. He was meeting people in the mall and sharing his faith without solicitation.

Bo was securely in the First Stage of the Christian walk. He was on fire for God and was eagerly learning what that meant through Bible study and sermon attendance. Like most folks in this stage, he was trying to clean up his life within his own strength and did not quite understand the spiritual warfare that was raging in his life. He was as Paul puts it (Hebrews 5:12–14), a babe living on the milk of the Word. Bo would often come to the group and be confused about scripture and would misinterpret its meaning. Bo's behavior of occasional falls to excess was not the thing that kept him in Stage One, it was the inability to apply the few things he had learned from scripture. He did not live with his wife in an understanding way, bringing her patiently along as a "weaker vessel." He was trying to take the spiritual leadership of his home but allowed his encouragement to become demands leading to arguments. When things didn't work out the way the preacher said, he would escape through carnal means.

Bo started to advance to the Second Stage which is actually the only bad stage of the three. More on that stage later, but to finish Bo's story, his zeal for the Lord was superficial and was not enough to guide him and his family through the valley of addiction and unfulfilled expectations. Yes, the men in the group prayed for him, with him, and over him, and he was very transparent when confessing to the group, but he didn't submit to the most important lesson of the Christian walk, pick up your cross daily and follow Him. He didn't understand that to do this you must put the needs of others before yours. He had most of the necessary words but could not go beyond the outward behavior and submit to an inner change. Bo and his wife did not love each other as Christ loved the Church, which resulted in affairs and the end of their marriage. I still see Bo every now and then, and he works a menial job, with frequent stays in jail, and his children have drug addictions as well. He will still praise the Lord and say he's blessed, but I wonder if he has ever made it out of the First Stage.

While in my teen years, I knew another young man two years older than I, actually a friend of my older brother. We used to hang out together because he had his license, and I did not. He was a normal teenager, carnal in nature and given to vice. He attended a student worship service for reasons I don't recall and became on fire for the Lord. Since I didn't know much about salvation then, I didn't recognize if he claimed salvation or not. I know that he spent several nights a week meeting with Christian groups, and I noted how much his life changed. I remember being happy for him because he seemed so happy and committed. I was a little convicted, because he was turning into what I knew I should be. Not long after that, I noticed him cooling off a bit, and then my family moved from the area, and I never spoke with him again. I have recently connected with him on Facebook to find that he is doing very well but there is no evidence of a spiritual walk. That's not to say that he is not saved, but if he had maintained the fire I saw early in his walk, there would be some evidence on Facebook. I don't post much on Facebook, but friends that connect with me can tell I'm a Christian by the things that I post and more importantly, by the things that I don't. This friend was another example of Stage One people. They start out on fire, and you would think they would beat down the Devil single-handedly. Most people stay on a growing walk and make it to Stage Two but some never do. Like my friend, they cool off and fall away. For those that never make it to the next stage, they usually find themselves looking for something that is carnal, temporal, and without cost. Something by which they can profit. When they discover the walk involves time, study, submission, and building a relationship with Jesus, they lose interest.

As I mentioned before, my salvation experience took place over time, but I do remember going through the First Stage. I had been religious my entire life and thought of church as a place to go and fulfill my obligation to attend and experience the ritual of participating in a religious service. I recall learning Bible stories but not learning exactly what they meant and how they pointed to a Messiah, Jesus Christ, that would save me from my sin and enable me to have everlasting life. I always believed the salvation story but never accepted it as the gospel that would be my redemption. I was still trying to be good enough to go to heaven. Since I didn't know God's standard for holiness in all cases, I never knew for sure if I was measuring up. When I gave in to the Holy Spirit's leading and gave my life to Christ and trusted Him and His blood on the cross for my salvation, His Word began to come alive to me. I understood more, I applied more, and I hungered for more. I gained new power in my fight against sin. I wanted to sin less but I still held on to those things that brought me pleasure. Most of those things reflected a reluctance to guard my heart and mind against things that were unholy. I felt connected to the body of Christ and started to become involved, serving where my youth would allow. I changed my perspective on church from an obligation to a privilege. Prior to my salvation I was one of those people who liked to go to church on Sunday but if I missed one or two, or twenty services, no big deal. I thought I could worship God on a golf course or at home in a quiet moment, which one can, but does one? I didn't.

"And let us consider one another in order to stir up love and good works, not forsaking the assembling together, as is the manner of some, but exhorting one another, and so much the more as you see the Day approaching." (Hebrews 10:25)

Stage Two

The good and bad news is that I made it to the Second Stage. The person that stays on fire and continues to grow in the Word will have to go through the Second Stage. Everyone that

I have observed have similar characteristics. Their zeal for the Lord drives them to learn more, so they are very intentional about their Bible study. Their growth in the Word takes them to a place where they know enough to be dangerous, and that's what they become, dangerous. Once you know the Word of God, you expect everyone to follow every jot and tittle. The problem is that no one does, because no one can—that's why we need a Savior. The good people in this stage forget that they themselves don't meet this standard but they focus on the non-compliance of others. Even this is a noble attempt at spreading God's Word and standing for righteousness, but the method becomes one of self-righteousness and makes for a bad witness.

"And why do you look at the speck in your brother's eye, but do not consider the plank in your own eye?" (Matthew 7:3)

I have heard many well-meaning Christians speak to people very harshly as they tell them what the Bible says about their actions, activities, or attitudes. As I look at Jesus' life, I noticed that He condemned sin, but not the sinner. Consider the prostitute that was to be stoned at the gate. After He saved her life, He told her to go and sin no more. The only people that He spoke harshly to were the Pharisees and the merchants that were selling in the temple. Why should we do differently? It is a subtle difference between acknowledging sin for what it is, yet understanding that the one committing the sin is no worse than the rest of us that sin. It is critical to "hate the sin, but love the sinner."

The people in the Second Stage now see faults in others and take it upon themselves to call them out in an attempt to restore righteousness. There's no doubt that we are called to be holy, for He is holy, but the method of our sanctification can be a stumbling block for those that may be searching. If they see a hateful, mean-spirited attitude, they will be repelled from emulating a life surrendered to Christ and wonder if Christianity is even something they want to learn more about. Remember, you are trying to share Christ with people who have not yet accepted Him and are seeking truth. They must obtain *justification* before they can work on *sanctification*.

Now, please don't make the mistake of thinking I'm suggesting watering down the gospel message or reduce our beliefs to the relativism that is common in churches today. I'm not talking about tickling the ears of the seekers or not following the Word of God. I'm talking about the method in which we share our faith.

If someone expresses a belief that is contrary to God's Word, some Christians may respond in a manner such as...

"That is a lie straight from the pit of hell!"

This may well be true, but it's also the very kind of attitude that keeps people from embracing the gospel in the first place. As I stated before, people are looking for a reason not to believe, and you may have just given them one. I would recommend a response that gives the appearance that you are trying to reason with them rather than condemn them.

"You know, I don't see that belief as honoring to God, or at least from what I know of God from the Bible."

Then you can see where that statement takes the conversation. At least the conversation may continue.

The message is basically the same, but the method may be much more successful.

Second Stage people also tend to move toward legalism as well. I think it's because they learn God's Word and want to live by it, but they are only developed enough to know the *word* of the Word but not the *spirit* of the Word. It takes a great deal of prayerful study to not only know what the Word says but also what it means. It's a great thing to apply God's Word to your life as you learn it, but many things cannot be properly applied until you know the Word in full. Many years ago, I recall applying the qualifications as a deacon from 1 Timothy 3:5: *"For if a man does not know how to rule his own house, how will he take care of the church of God?"*

I had told the other deacons in my church that my brother-in-law was living at my house but that he was not saved and did not attend church. I asked if this would disqualify me as a Deacon, applying 1 Timothy 3:5. They asked how old he was. When I told them he was 41, they laughed and assured me he is responsible for his spiritual condition and that would certainly not disqualify me. As you can see, I was legalistic with my interpretation of scripture.

This is an example of how Second Stage people can appear petty and self-righteous to a non-believer. The reason it is important that you guard against remaining in this stage and recognize people dwelling in this stage is because they can very innocently impede your witness by debating peripheral topics in the company of someone with whom you are trying to witness. No one wants to hear two Christians duking it out over inconsistent doctrine, unless, of course, they want to use the argument to discredit the faith.

Sharing your faith means sharing not only the gospel but also your beliefs and your interpretations of scripture. It's healthy to discuss different interpretations with a brother or sister in Christ, but not if it turns into a vain argument in front of those who desperately need to see the love of Jesus.

I've been asked a few times if it is spiritually wrong to play the lottery. In my Second Stage days I would have answered something like...

"Yes, the Bible refers to this as sordid gain, and no true Christian should participate in such a Satanic practice."

Well, now I know that such a response will be appreciated by other Second Stage people, but they are already saved, and I'm trying to witness to people that still need Jesus, and they will most likely be turned away by such a statement. My new answer is...

"Well, I can only tell you what God has spoken to me. He has told me that He has already provided what He wants me to have, and it is much more than enough. Trying to get rich off the lottery is like telling Him that His blessings are not enough, and I am going to get what I want on my own."

"But is the lottery wrong?"

"That's something you'll have to ask God and see what He says."

I think this response puts the focus on my relationship with the Lord and not on the legalistic judgment of the behavior of others. It sends the message of "trust God" rather than "the lottery is bad." This gets to be easier as we learn to see people and their actions as people on a spiritual journey and that all of us are on a different phase of that journey. When you realize this, you are entering into the Third Stage.

Stage Three

The Third Stage is the place where mature Christians realize that they are no better than anyone else and that any holiness they may have demonstrated was done so through the power and mercy of God and the equipping of the Holy Spirit. They

remember when they were unsaved and in the First or Second
Stages to the point they are thankful they are more concerned
with their personal relationship with God than with the trans-
gressions of others. I like to keep one thought in mind when
comparing myself to others. I am not any better than anyone
else; I'm just redeemed. By God's standard, my sin is no better
than those of Hitler, Chairman Mao, the sinner I work with,
or the pervert down the street, but when God sees me, He sees
the blood of Jesus that covers me.

*"But as many as received Him, to them He gave the right
to become children of God, to those who believe in His name."*
(John 1:12)

I always feared scriptures such as 1 Corinthians 6:9–10:

*"Do you not know that the unrighteous will not inherit the
kingdom of God? Do not be deceived. Neither fornicators, nor
idolaters, nor adulterers, nor homosexuals, nor sodomites, nor
thieves, nor covetous, nor drunkards, nor revilers, nor extortion-
ers will inherit the kingdom of God."*

Wait a minute, I do some of these things. Am I not saved?

Then we must read verse 11.

*"And such were some of you. But you were washed, but you
were sanctified, but you were justified in the name of the Lord
Jesus and by the Spirit of our God."*

It took me many years to understand that I may do those
things, but I am not those things. I am a blood-washed,
redeemed, chosen child of the Most High God, and that is how
He sees me. Hallelujah!

And it was not through anything I had done, but only
through His mercy and grace (Ephesians 2:8–9), so I do not
merit the high ranking of judging others by their deeds. The
Stage Three person understands that when they see a brother

or sister fall, or exhibit a sinful act or lifestyle, they should see it as an act against God's Word, but the act does not make them any less a child of God. Their sin does not make the Stage Three person any more a child of God, or any more loved by Him. The attitude of the Stage Three person would be something like…

"Lord, I see this person struggling with this sin. I ask you to free them that they may turn away from it. Send me that they may see Christ in my life and be encouraged to repent. Give me the words to disciple them. I praise You that I have not fallen to this sin but make me mindful of the sins I have chosen for myself, both with and without a struggle. I can only claim the blood of Jesus for their forgiveness. May You receive all the glory for a change in this person's life and in mine. In the name of Jesus, I pray. Amen."

This attitude agrees with God in several ways:

- You agree that what you are seeing is against God's Word.
- You agree that only God can defeat the flesh and release the grip of this sin.
- You agree that you need to be the one to come alongside of this person.
- You agree that it is only by His grace that you do not struggle with that particular sin, or maybe you do.
- You agree that you have sin in your life and are justified only by His grace.
- You agree that if this person repents, God is to receive the glory.
- You are asking in the name of Jesus with the right motive.

You can see how this attitude is better than the Stage Two person, such as…

"Ohhhhhh, you're siniiiiiiing!"

Here is a short list of characteristics I've observed in a Stage Three person:

- Does not seek positions of influence in the local church body but serves when called by God.
- Seeks God's calling for service and says, "yes."
- Does not fill a task or position just because there is a need.
- Seeks God's will in every decision.
- Applies God's will and Word to job and family situations.
- Is not ashamed of the gospel of Christ.
- Strives to be above reproach in word and deed.
- Strives for holiness, guarding their heart against exposure to sin.
- Does not define people by the sins they commit but as saints that struggle just as they do.
- Knows that all blessings come from above and that God is to be praised and glorified for anything good that happens in their life.
- Knows that their skills and abilities are gifts from God, and therefore their achievements are for His glory.
- Know how to be in the world but not of the world.
- Longs for heaven but maintains a burden for the lost.
- Can recognize spiritual warfare and knows how to fight.
- Has an endless desire to learn God's Word and draw closer to Him.
- Submits to authority God has placed over them and shows proper respect.

- Guards their tongue, not speaking ill of others, not given to profanity.
- Recognizes heretical teaching and rejects it, publicly when necessary.
- Takes advantage of opportunities to share the gospel.
- Believes in and utilizes the purpose and power of prayer.
- Walks by faith.

This is by no means an exhaustive list, but I have exhausted myself in putting it together. Hopefully you can get the idea of what a Stage Three person is like.

Writing this chapter makes me reflect on where I truly am in this journey. I would assess myself as being at the end of Stage Two and slightly into Stage Three. I exhibit some of the characteristics listed above but come severely short of many of them.

Then why did I write this book?

I wrote this book to share ideas and experiences that I believe God has given me to help people who want to winsomely and safely share their faith at their workplace and in the community. I am trying to be transparent in saying that I am not "securely" in Stage Three because like many, I have falls. I struggle to be in the world but not of the world. I pursue many activities and hobbies that do not include sharing the gospel. I love playing music. I play in the praise band at times and often play and sing hymns when I perform, but I also like to play classic pop, country, and bluegrass music. I love college basketball and football. The basketball thing is not a sin because I graduated from the University of Kentucky, therefore have no choice (LOL). I am not given to many vices. I do not drink, smoke, chew, cuss, gamble, or tell dirty jokes, however, I am not as committed to holiness as I should be. I watch many things on TV that are not honoring to God. What's worse, I enjoy them. My mind is generally filled with various lusts of the flesh. I think about having expensive sports cars, musical instruments, winning the lottery (even though I do not play it), and yes, even SEX. My most egregious sin may be my passive-aggressive anger management failures. By the grace of God I rarely act out on them but the thoughts that manifest in your head begin in your heart. My heart is wicked; I need a savior.

Many will say:

"Well, that's just being human. You are too hard on yourself. Nobody's perfect."

An elderly man whom I respect greatly once said that to me. I had to rebuke him asking him to please not discourage me from striving for God's plumb line. I know I will never get there, but I need to continue to strive. The key to the Stage Three person is to continue to strive without judging others as they do the same. No matter where you are in this journey, there will always be someone who is closer to His standard than you and someone who is further away.

CHAPTER

6

SUMMARY

To review, this book is an encouragement for sharing your faith in the workplace, and it gives some strategies and ideas on how to do it while minimizing your legal vulnerability. I say "minimize" because you should be aware that no matter what your legal rights may be, someone is going to take offense at your sharing even if they are not the person to whom you are talking. Our society is becoming less and less tolerant of people publicly displaying their spiritual beliefs, especially Christian beliefs, and you cannot depend on a legal system or company policy to protect your rights. Knowing this, if you still choose to share the gospel at work "in and out of season," these ideas can help answer questions you may have like "What if this happens?" or "What if they say_____?", or "How do I start the interaction?" or "What if they are not interested in talking about it?"

Here are some summary points that may help you index through the book and get specific ideas.

- Remember you are at your job to be a witness; this is your mission field, not just a job.
- Do your job as if unto the Lord.
- Respect authority.

- Show Christ in your life to the point people want to know why you are different.
- You may be the only Jesus that some people ever see.
- Be prepared to give a reason for the hope that resides in you.
- 2 Timothy 2:15. Read it, know it, live it!
- Know the difference between a seeker and a non-seeker and know how to interact with both.
- Maintain your witness at all times and don't enter into "vain arguments." The calling is to share the gospel, not win an argument.
- Don't feel you have to answer every theological question. Stick to the gospel.
- Be pleasant in your approach but don't compromise the gospel or the Word.
- Recognize when it's time to shake the dust from your feet.
- Remember, you can't save anyone; you can only tell. God doesn't need your help, but He wants your submission and obedience.
- Christians can sometimes present an obstacle for sharing your faith.
- Be prayed-up and ask for a heart for the lost.
- The battle belongs to the Lord.

I hope there are some ideas in this book that will help you in your witness. I'm just another guy with an opinion and some experience, and most of all, a love for the Lord. Please treat this information as "accept or reject." There may be parts you can use and some with which you vehemently disagree. That's fine, I generally don't trust the wisdom of people that agree with everything I say. I have, however, shared these ideas with a few people at work, and they have found them to be very interesting, so I decided to write them down in a book for the benefit of others.

May God bless you for your willingness to share the gospel at work and in your community. May He go out before you and ready the hearts of seekers and non-seekers to receive the Word He has given you to share. May He keep you from harm and tribulation as you share, or may He give you the strength to withstand the consequences of doing His kingdom work. May He protect you from the darts of the evil one who will try to stop you in your efforts by distracting you with adversity. May you see the fruit of your labor as people accept Jesus Christ as their personal Lord and Savior and win for themselves the prize of eternal life. May Jesus Christ be glorified in your work. May you receive crowns in heaven for your obedience.

"Go therefore and make disciples of all the nations, baptizing them in the name of the Father and of the Son and of the Holy Spirit, teaching them to observe all things that I have commanded you; and lo, I am with you always, even to the end of the age." (Mathew 28:19–20)

Bibliography

The Holy Bible, New King James Version (Nashville, TN: Thomas Nelson, Inc.), 1982.

New American Standard Exhaustive Concordance of the Bible (La Habra, CA: The Lockman Foundation), 1981.

Made in the USA
Middletown, DE
15 November 2021

52515640R00060